PRAISE FOR

BILLY
GRAHAM
AN ORDINARY MAN
AND HIS EXTRAORDINARY GOD

"This is a book you must read because this is a man you should know. Through him, millions have come to know the God who loves them and gives hope. And this God, the God who made the universe and you and me, loves you. He loves you deeply and dearly. There are so many of us who loved Billy Graham, myself included, and Lon is someone who knew and loved Billy and had the privilege of serving by his side. His is a unique perspective into a unique man whose message will impact your unique life."

—DR. MICHAEL OH, Global Executive Director and CEO, Lausanne Movement

"This is a book that is about an extraordinary God who spoke through and is displayed himself through Billy Graham. In chapter after chapter, you will read about how you also can experience a close relationship with God."

—STEVE DOUGLASS, President, Campus Crusade for Christ/Cru

"Lon Allison's winsome biography about Billy Graham is much more than a biography. Not only do we get a look at Billy's ordinary life which became an extraordinary life, we get portraits of Jesus Christ in almost every chapter. Mr. Graham never wanted the attention to be on him. He wanted Jesus and his Gospel to shine. In this book, you will see Jesus shine forth, and it will be an encouragement to Christians and a helpful explanation for non-Christians."

—ED STETZER, PhD, Billy Graham Chair of Church, Mission and Evangelism,
Wheaton College

"I woke at 5:00 AM this morning and read the entire book! I love good biographies and this book is no exception. Lon Allison explores the extraordinary life of Billy Graham: his roots, conversion, ministry, family life and even his regrets. You will be drawn to the person of Jesus, who fills every chapter. I highly commend this book to you."

—BECKY MANLEY PIPPERT, author of Out of the Saltshaker and into the World

"As a lover and collector of biographies, I am thrilled with Lon Allison's new book on Billy Graham. There are already a dozen biographies of Graham on my shelf, but Lon's contribution is a unique profile of this great evangelist and America's pastor. And that's because Lon himself is a passionate evangelist and pastor. He gets Billy Graham. Lon loves to share the gospel, which is woven into this biography with gripping clarity. This is a book to read for yourself and to purchase for your friends!"

—JIM L. NICODEM, Senior Pastor, Christ Community Church, St. Charles, IL;
author of Prayer Coach

"I love this book! Lon, who personally knew Billy Graham in both formal and informal settings, is just the right man to introduce us to the human side of the famous evangelist. Yes, there were the large crusades, fiery preaching, and press conferences. But there is also that other side of Billy, relaxing in a chair, visiting, asking questions, and encouraging all whom he met. Once again you will be impressed by Billy's humility, his deferential attitude toward others, and his down-to-earth view of the world. No matter how much you have read about Billy Graham you will discover this is a delightful page-turner. Read it and pass it along."

—DR. ERWIN W. LUTZER, Pastor Emeritus, The Moody Church, author of *Rescuing the Gospel*

"Billy Graham's recent graduation to the presence of the Lord provides the perfect chance to reflect on the life lessons, faith, vision, and passion for the Gospel that characterized his life and can characterize the lives of all followers of Jesus. Mr. Graham modeled a refreshing humility and confidence in the power of the Good News to radically change lives. He devoted his life to a simple yet powerful message, and Lon Allison shares the belief that nothing in life is more important than communicating this message far and wide. Read this book and be inspired to follow in the footsteps of one of the great ones."

—KEVIN PALAU, President, Luis Palau Association

"With an insider's perspective, Lon has captured Billy Graham's relentless commitment to evangelism, heartbeat of grace-filled relationships, and God-trusting enormous vision. Lon shows through his own life how Dr. Graham's timeless core is an inspiring model to study and emulate."

—DR. ROGER PARROTT, President, Belhaven University

"A great introduction to one of the defining figures of our times. My friend and fellow evangelist, Lon Allison, has given us an honest and insightful portrayal of Billy Graham that authentically conveys both the man and the power of his message."

—J. JOHN, Reverend Canon and Evangelist, England

"My two favorite evangelists of this generation are Billy Graham and Lon Allison. I believe it's no accident they had a long partnership in ministry and relationship. Not only will you get great insights from this book about Billy Graham, you'll get great insights as well about how to represent the Christian faith in our generation with class and power."

—RAY JOHNSTON, Founding and Senior Pastor, Bayside Churches, California

"There are many exhaustive books on Dr. Billy Graham. What makes this one special is its unique accessibility. Lon covers the contours of Dr. Graham's life, while finding the applicability for our own. Yes, you will learn the life story of Dr. Graham, but you will also learn his life motivation—giving himself unreservedly, so that people like us, from all walks of life, from all over the world, would know we are loved by God. Through this book, as you take an interest in Dr. Graham, you cannot help but take encouragement knowing God knows you and loves you."

—GARY WALTER, President, The Evangelical Covenant Church

BILLY
GRAHAM

AN ORDINARY MAN
AND HIS EXTRAORDINARY GOD

LON ALLISON

Foreword by Dr. Leighton Ford and Jean Graham Ford

PARACLETE PRESS
BREWSTER, MASSACHUSETTS

2018 First Printing

Billy Graham: An Ordinary Man and His Extraordinary God

Copyright © 2018 by Lonnie J. Allison

ISBN 978-1-64060-087-4

Unless otherwise noted, quotations from Holy Scripture are taken from the Holy Bible, New International Version®, NIV®. Copyright © 1973, 1978, 1984, 2011 by Biblica, Inc.™ Used by permission of Zondervan. All rights reserved worldwide. www.zondervan.com. The "NIV" and "New International Version" are trademarks registered in the United States Patent and Trademark Office by Biblica, Inc.™

Scripture quotations marked (NLT) are taken from the Holy Bible, New Living Translation, copyright ©1996, 2004, 2015 by Tyndale House Foundation. Used by permission of Tyndale House Publishers, Inc., Carol Stream, Illinois 60188. All rights reserved.

Scripture quotations marked (ESV) are taken from The ESV® Bible (The Holy Bible, English Standard Version®), copyright © 2001 by Crossway, a publishing ministry of Good News Publishers. Used by permission. All rights reserved.

Scripture quotations marked (CEV) are taken from the Contemporary English Version © 1991, 1992, 1995 by American Bible Society. Used by Permission.

The Paraclete Press name and logo (dove on cross) are trademarks of Paraclete Press, Inc.

Library of Congress Cataloging-in-Publication Data
Names: Allison, Lon (Lon J.), 1952- author.
Title: Billy Graham : an ordinary man and his extraordinary god / Lon Allison
; foreword by Dr. Leighton Ford and Jean Graham Ford.
Description: Brewster, MA : Paraclete Press, Inc., 2018. | Includes
bibliographical references.
Identifiers: LCCN 2018008555 | ISBN 9781640600874 (hardcover)
Subjects: LCSH: Graham, Billy, 1918-2018. | Evangelists—United
States—Biography.
Classification: LCC BV3785.G69 A75 2018 | DDC 269/.2092 [B]—dc23
LC record available at https://lccn.loc.gov/2018008555

10 9 8 7 6 5 4 3 2 1

Published by Paraclete Press
Brewster, Massachusetts
www.paracletepress.com

Printed in the United States of America

CONTENTS

May God use these pages to point you
not to Billy Graham, but to Jesus Christ,
the one I have always sought to serve.[1]

You have no idea how sick I get of the name
Billy Graham, and how wonderful and thrilling
the name Christ sounds to my ears.[2]

—BILLY GRAHAM

FOREWORD

This book is about an ordinary man. It is also written for ordinary readers, not scholars, historians, or theologians. And we are so glad for that—because Billy always had a heart for ordinary people. You may remember him, perhaps vaguely, as a preacher to large crowds, a personality on television, an admired celebrity. But who was he? What did he stand for? I overheard two young people talking and one asked, "What is this Billy Graham about anyway?" The other replied, "I think he's some old guy who wants everyone to be good"!

This book will tell you what he was about. Who he was. What his message was. And how his message can bring new hope and meaning to your life. As an artist friend, a relative of his, said, "He looked as if he knew something. Something he had to share." And he did.

We can still picture him when he spoke to a crowd: standing tall, humble, with piercing blue eyes, hands clutching a Bible, jabbing them out to make a point. His voice was clear and penetrating, like the whistle of a train on an early morning, with a hint of thunder.

But to us the personal Billy is as real as the public preacher. There were not two Billy Grahams. Just one. He was as real and genuine in person as he was on the platform.

I (Jeanie) remember when I was about five and my big brother put me in his goat wagon and got the goat to pull me out to the garden to pick vegetables. And when I had polio, he had just made the long drive to Chicago, and when he heard I was sick he turned around and came straight home to care for me.

I (Leighton) remember when I was seventeen and he came to speak at a youth rally in my home city in Canada. I was the leader and was sure all our friends would come forward to give their lives to follow Jesus. Only one did. I was so disappointed. But Billy put an arm around my shoulder and told me he would pray for me, and if I stayed humble God would use me.

His tall frame is gone now, his voice silenced. But his presence is still very real.

We are so glad that Lon Allison was asked to write this book. He is the right person to do it. Lon himself is a gifted evangelist. He has a deep passion to make Christ real and available to people. As the director for years of the Billy Graham Center at Wheaton College he knows firsthand how wide and deep the influence of Billy has been.

As you read, our wish and hope is that the extraordinary God, who used this ordinary man, will use this book to make his extraordinary love very real and compelling to you.

—LEIGHTON AND JEAN FORD
Charlotte, North Carolina

INTRODUCTION

I'm a reluctant witness when it comes to writing about Billy Graham. I am privileged to know him and to have visited with him several times, beginning in the last decade of his public ministry. I also got to know many of his closest team members and some of the family. Even as I sit here writing I think of them with much fondness and respect. They remind me of the words of the psalmist who said,

> I say of the holy ones who are in the land,
>> "They are the noble ones in whom is all my delight."
>>> (Ps. 16:3)

My bird's-eye view came from serving as the executive director of the Billy Graham Center at Wheaton College in Wheaton, Illinois. Those were fifteen wonderful years. I am full of memories and reflections from what I learned.

So, why am I reluctant to write of him? Because he emphatically disliked attention. He would often quote from Isaiah 48:11, stating that God "will not yield [his] glory to another." He feared people would focus on him more than on the God who created him, saved him, and called him to serve the world with the great message of his Lord Jesus Christ. For instance, in 1996 he visited the campus of Wheaton College, his alma mater, and was led on a tour of the "new," revised Billy Graham Center Museum. First off, he didn't like it called the Billy Graham Center Museum. Why? He'd felt the original rendition, which opened in 1980, was too focused on his life and not enough on the work of God operating through many others in the evangelization of America. Further, he feared there was too much Billy Graham and too little Jesus Christ in the story the museum presented. So as he completed his tour of the newly revised exhibits he was asked if he now liked it better. One of his friends told me this story and showed me the exact spot where Billy responded. His words were few but poignant: "there is still too much Billy Graham here."

Thus I am reluctant to offer yet another version of the Billy Graham story, knowing he would have frowned on such a thing. He really would not want it. On top of that, several excellent books on his life and ministry have been written, and a few of them in recent years. Many are by trained historians with the expertise that only those in that field have mastered. Is another book needed, and by a nonhistorian like me? No, not really. Yet both the publisher who first approached me and a couple of close friends argued that I might be perfect for another Billy Graham book as we neared the centennial year of his life. Why? Because an observant eyewitness who would focus just as much on the message Mr. Graham preached as on Billy himself might be helpful.

I know it would please Billy more for a book about him to take such an approach. As one of my young friends, Johnnie Moore, said, "Lon, you have to write this because Billy made Jesus bigger." That sold me. If I have anything to offer, it is to look at his life from a slightly different point of view. I'd like to tell Mr. Graham's story, but always pointing to the Good News or gospel about Jesus that was the core purpose of his life. I'll explain more about this Good News or gospel in a moment. But my take on Mr. Graham is that in every role of his life he was consumed with the desire to be obedient, with God's strength, so he might display the life of Christ. Friends who knew him far better than I did say it is so too.

Thus I'll be talking about Mr. Graham but always pointing to Jesus, who made Billy Graham the man he was. I recall the story of the preacher visiting a church as a guest speaker. When he stepped up to the pulpit there was a brass plaque on the pulpit facing him. It simply said, "Preacher, we wish to see Jesus." If you will allow, I will therefore write about Mr. G. (as we often called him), but more about Jesus, who worked so powerfully in him.

Now, as promised, let me define a word that will be used a lot in the book. It's the word *gospel*. *Gospel* is an Old English word that means "good spell or story." Often today it is also called good news or good message. It is used a lot, but always means the same thing. It is the good news or good message or good story about God. That's it in a nutshell. The gospel is about God. The God Billy Graham believed in is the God of the Bible, who, we are told, is the only God and is distinctly three persons in the same God. He is the Father, the Son (Jesus), and the Holy Spirit. Three distinct persons as one God.

The essence of the gospel is that God the Father loved humankind so very much he sent his only Son, Jesus, to die for our sins and then, three days later, to rise to new life so he could live in all who seek him by the Holy Spirit. In that person of the Spirit, he promises to be with us and in us always. Because of these great acts of God, people can experience three tremendous benefits, which is why it is such gospel—such Good News. First, we can know him personally. He is no longer distant and otherworldly. We can actually experience God living in our own hearts. The second benefit is to receive forgiveness for all our evil thoughts, words, and deeds from our past, our present, and our future. We are completely forgiven, and not on the basis of our goodness (because we aren't good enough), but by his perfect goodness (because Jesus *was* good enough). Not only are we forgiven for our badness, but because he lives in us, he starts transforming us into the good people we've always wanted to be. Finally, we receive the gift of eternal life in heaven when we die. And like forgiveness, heaven can't be earned, but is freely given.

I hope you can now see why this is such good news and why Billy and so many others, including me, have given our lives to tell people this gospel. I am quite sure that anything good we witness in Mr. Graham's life, he would readily credit to the gospel of the living God working in him. Further, any failures and even sins we find in his history, whether it be in his personal life or ministry, he'd readily attribute to those times when instead of relying on God, he depended instead on himself. Whenever people try to do God's work for him without depending completely on God to do it, there is failure.

My prayer is that this book will be read by a generation that has never heard of Billy Graham. When I asked my twenty-six-year-old musician-artist son if his friends would know of Billy Graham he said, "Dad, they know more about Bill Graham, one of the first producers of the music of the 1960s, than they will Billy Graham." So, it is for them that I write. I also write for those who are broadly attached to the Christian faith, and for those who have had only a small or short brush with faith in their lives. Billy influenced everyone from Catholics and Lutherans to Bible church evangelicals and Assemblies of God charismatics. As I hope you will hear clearly in what follows, he touched people like me with very little religious background. He was the "pastor to presidents" and a spiritual guide to celebrities. But more than everything else, he was a friend of Jesus and passionately devoted to telling Jesus's story to everyone he possibly could in all the world.

FIRST IMPRESSIONS

God blesses those who are humble,
for they will inherit the whole earth.
—*Matthew 5:5 (NLT)*

———

I am not a great preacher and
I don't claim to be a great preacher. . . .
I'm just an ordinary preacher,
just communicating the Gospel
in the best way I know how.

—BILLY GRAHAM[3]

L et me tell you about when I first met with Billy Graham in person. This story illustrates a bit of who the man was. It was a summer Sunday night in 1998. I flew to Ottawa, Canada, to meet with him. I was at that time being considered for the role of director of the Billy Graham Center at Wheaton College in Illinois, and Billy had to approve me for the task. Those in leadership at the college had told me the meeting was mostly a formality, since the search committee had already voted to call me, but still, they wanted Billy to be consulted. Ottawa was the location for our meeting because that's where Billy was. It was the last night of his crusade in that city.

I was nervous as they led me to a private hospitality room that Sunday afternoon in the lower recesses of the great Ottawa stadium. Billy often met with dignitaries, church leaders, major donors, celebrities, and the like prior to going out to preach, and I was taken to a room loaded with fruits, cheeses, cold drinks, cookies, and all manner of good things to sustain me until I was summoned. Other people were there as well. I think one of the people was the mayor of Ottawa. Others were business leaders and a leading Ottawa pastor or two. One by one or in groups, they were taken in to talk with Graham. When none of them returned to the green room, I assumed that after you met with Billy you were ushered somewhere else to see the spectacle about to commence, namely, the crusade meeting. Soon, I was alone and waiting in the room.

Finally, the door of the suite opened and the director of North American Crusades for the Billy Graham Evangelistic Association (BGEA), Dr. Sterling Huston, entered. Dr. Huston was the man responsible for the crusade that was going on above us. He was also the leader of the selection committee for the new director of the Graham Center. Sterling was one of the finest Christian gentlemen I ever met. He smiled and asked if I was ready. I said, quaveringly, "Sure," but I was increasingly nervous. I already realized I was in some kind of rarified air and was out of my league.

Ever since I had first heard about Billy Graham, and seen him preach for the first time as a freshman in college, I had been in awe. I did not come from a Christian family. I was not raised in any kind of a church. But in my later high school years I heard the gospel at a critical time in life and responded to the invitation to commit my life to Christ. I had been intensely lonely and suffered chronic guilt from life failures even though I was only sixteen, but when I heard of God's love and forgiveness of my sins, I jumped into Christ's forgiving arms. My life began changing slowly, and I began to sense that God could truly forgive even me. I started telling friends what I'd found. My irresistible urge to know God and Christ began to grow to an urge to tell people what I'd found. So, two years later, as a freshman in college, there I was leading a whole busload of kids to see and hear, for the first time, this man named Billy Graham. Fifty thousand people or more were present in the Oakland Coliseum that night in 1971. I was amazed. Where had they all come from? Were this many people looking for God to help them, just as I had been? When Graham invited anyone seeking God to come to the front of the stadium, my amazement reached astonishment. They just kept coming and coming and coming. Now, thirty years later, I was going to meet him in person.

As Dr. Huston and I left the green room and headed down a hallway, my anxiety increased yet another notch. I had been with the mayor of Ottawa and other Canadian leaders in the hospitality room, but I was a stranger to them, as they were to me. Now, as we walked the long, dimly lit hallway, I saw several large men in business suits, each with an earpiece, looking quite serious, watching me pass by. They did not smile. They were hired security. I remember feeling uncomfortable around all the pomp and circumstance, and wondered if this is what it is like to meet a president or a king. I also wondered, *Is all this really necessary for meeting a Christian speaker?* Finally, we approached another door. Standing outside was another large man in a suit who looked about my age. He was the final checkpoint guard, I guessed. He was not smiling either, but he wasn't quite as scary as the rest of the security detail. Dr. Huston stopped and said to the man, "Franklin, this is Lon Allison. He's here to meet your father and talk about the Graham Center position." That was my introduction to Franklin Graham, who was being a good son by watching over his eighty-year-old father from outside the door. Franklin smiled and we shook hands; then he opened the door.

The room wasn't nearly as nice as the hospitality suite. In fact, it appeared to be part of the backstage to the Ottawa stadium floor. There were two high-backed chairs with a small table, as I recall, and there might have been a small carpet under the chairs. There was no pretense in this room, no grandeur, no armed guards, no cookies and cheese or Perrier. There was only an elderly white-haired man sitting in one of the chairs. Sterling looked at the man and said, "Bill"—if you really knew him well, you could call him Bill—"this is Lon Allison." Then, Billy spoke. I will never forget what he said: "I've been waiting to meet you." I didn't expect those words. He went on to say that "they," meaning the search committee, "tell me I have to sign off on the next director of the Wheaton Center." Even then he refused to call it the Billy Graham Center. For fifteen years, or whenever I spoke with him, it was never the Billy Graham Center, just simply "the Wheaton Center." Then he added, "I don't think it necessary I approve you, but I am glad to meet you."

Billy went on to ask about my family. He wanted to know about my wife and children. I didn't expect that either. Then he talked a bit about his family. Wasn't he far too busy to talk with me, particularly at that moment? Well over twenty thousand people were pouring into the hockey stadium above us to hear him speak. And yet, he had time to talk with me about my family. We chatted for five or ten minutes about our personal lives. Then we discussed, as I recall, his love for "the

Wheaton Center" and for Wheaton College, where it was located, and how he hoped it would be a place where many younger leaders would be trained to declare the gospel to the world.

At some point during our conversation, which was now about twenty minutes long, Dr. Huston said to Billy, "Bill, I wanted you to know that Lon earned his doctorate at Gordon-Conwell" (a seminary Mr. Graham also helped start, though I don't think I knew that at that time), "and Lon's thesis was on evangelistic preaching for the twenty-first century."

"It was?" Billy said. Then he put his hand on my shoulder and asked the question I will never forget. It was the last possible thing I ever thought he would ask me. He said, "Do you think you could teach me some things about preaching the gospel better?" Now, pause for a moment and allow that question to sink in. Here was Billy Graham asking me to help him preach better! I laughed out loud, absolutely flabbergasted. Billy Graham was asking me to help him preach the gospel better. It was unbelievable. For a quick second, I wondered if it was a backhanded joke between him and Dr. Huston. But Billy looked at me so seriously and honestly when he said it.* When I realized this was no joke, all I could come up with in response was something like, "No, sir, I don't think I could since most of my work in the field is predicated on your example." He said something else, but I didn't hear it. By then my head was spinning.

Billy Graham in person was such a contrast to the massiveness of the stadium, the surging crowds, the hospitality suite, the dignitaries

---

* Incidentally, I have the picture taken by Billy Graham's photographer, Russ Busby, at precisely that moment to prove this. In the photo, I am laughing as the greatest evangelistic preacher in the world, perhaps in all of church history, asks me to teach him how to be better at his craft.

and celebrities, and the security force. He was a somewhat frail and exceedingly kind man who listened more than he talked, asked about my family, and then asked me to teach him about preaching, when he was the best at it in the world. The contrast was shocking, stunning. Finally, he thanked me for coming and said he was sorry we couldn't talk longer, but that one of the performing artists had asked to see him about her marital problems before the crusade started. He said she was like a daughter to him and he hoped her marriage would be okay.

That was my first personal experience of this man Billy Graham. His gentleness was striking, his humility astonishing. How can one of the most famous leaders in the world be so gentle and humble? In a world where leaders lie, curse, exaggerate, hyperbolize, castigate others, and display narcissistic behavior, where did this guy come from? From another world, I think. He was from a different mold than the world in which we dwell. By the way, in case you are wondering, this was who he was every time I was with him over the next fifteen years. More importantly, those who knew him far better than I corroborated the experience I'd had. Billy Graham's most compelling character traits were gentleness and a humility that leaves you shaking your head in wonder.

So, how does such a gentle, humble person become one of the most famous and important people in the world? The Bible says, "Humble yourselves, therefore, under God's mighty hand, that he may lift you up in due time" (1 Pet. 5:6). I guess that's how.

Billy would tell you that what I witnessed had little to do with him. He would tell you that only Christ living in him could make him as he was that Sunday evening in Ottawa. He would tell you that he was not always like that and that his own life was still full of sinful tendencies. And he would mean it, and he would be right. But there was the spark of a new kind of person in him. The Bible says that "if anyone is in Christ, the new creation has come: The old has gone, the new is here! All this is from God, who reconciled us to himself through Christ" (2 Cor. 5:17–18). What I witnessed that night was a man who had embraced Christ and was being transformed as a result. He was looking more and more like Jesus all the time because Jesus was in him. There are some verses in the Bible where Jesus called people to come to him and experience his power and character when he was on earth. "Come to me, all you who are weary and burdened, and I will give you rest. . . . For I am gentle and humble in heart, and you will find rest for your souls. For my yoke is easy and my burden is light" (Matt. 11:28–30). Gentle and humble of heart was part of who Jesus was. I saw a trace of that in Mr. Graham that night.

Every person can be made new inside and to look more and more like Jesus. That is part of the gospel message. We are forgiven for our flaws and evil behaviors, thoughts, and words. We are given a new, second birth with God in us and his beauty and perfection placed in our hearts. That is part of the gospel Graham preached throughout the world. This is possible because of God's Son, who died for our sins because of his great love.

How does one receive this new birth? By humbly admitting that living your life on your terms has not helped you or anyone else very much. By telling God how sorry you are for the flaws and evil in your old life. And finally, asking him to give you the new life where he is the center and the leader of everything. He will give you rest. And he will start to make you new.

Perhaps some readers sense the need to do this right now even though we are only starting to tell the story of Billy Graham's life and message for today. If so, please do it. Let nothing stop you. God awaits, and he loves you.

TWO
HOW IT ALL BEGAN

Direct your children onto the right path,
and when they are older, they will not leave it.
—*Proverbs 22:6 (NLT)*

———

I learned to obey without questioning. Lying, cheating, stealing, and property destruction were foreign to me. I was taught that laziness was one of the worst evils and that there was dignity and honor in labor.

—BILLY GRAHAM[4]

Billy Graham's birth on November 7, 1918, was sandwiched between two historic geopolitical events. The Bolshevik Revolution in Russia began a year to the day before he was born, and the armistice that ended World War I was signed four days after his birth. These momentous events are in stark contrast with the stunning regularity of Billy Graham's birth and early life, which played out like a slice of early twentieth-century Americana. In his superb biography of Mr. Graham, Grant Wacker puts it this way: "Perhaps the most remarkable thing about Graham's childhood and early adolescence is how unremarkable they really were."[5]

Billy was born on a dairy farm only five miles outside of Charlotte, North Carolina. His father, William Graham Sr., owned three hundred acres and seventy-five dairy cows. His mother, Morrow, gave birth to four children. Billy remembers his parents as loving yet firm, committed to one another, their children, and the welfare of their community. Billy was the oldest child, followed by Catherine, Melvin, and Jeanie. Jeanie, the baby of the family, was thirteen years younger than Billy. His childhood home, built when Billy was nine, still stands at the entrance to what is now the Billy Graham Library in Charlotte. It stands there to remind us of the comfortable farmhouse in an idyllic setting in the American South, the place of Billy's childhood.

When I was a young boy my family would watch a TV show every Sunday night. It was broadcast in black and white, but I remember it in vivid color. I'm humming the theme song right now as I think about it. The show's title was *Lassie*. It was the story of a farm family, their little boy, Timmy, and a wonderful dog named Lassie. That's how I think of Mr. Graham's boyhood. It was Lassie-like. By the way, Billy loved his dogs just like Timmy loved Lassie.

His boyhood was marked with hard work on the farm, going to the public schools, and having lots of fun. He rose at 2:30 every morning and joined his father's workers milking cows. Billy had twenty cows to milk every morning and night. He learned well and was able to milk a single cow in five minutes. At 5:30 AM he joined the workers and his father for a farm breakfast cooked by his mother each day. He learned to enjoy his tasks, and the value of hard work remained a priority throughout life. Billy was also a good student in elementary school, receiving mostly A grades.[6] His mother gave him a love for reading, and he liked the stories of Robin Hood, Tarzan, and *The Hardy Boys*.

He loved baseball and played the game throughout his youth. He shook Babe Ruth's hand once. He dreamed of being a big-league player, but by high school his athletic prowess proved less than he'd hoped. He was a substitute on his high school team, rather than a first-stringer.

His family would on occasion take brief two- or three-day vacations. The work of the farm prohibited them from longer retreats. The most memorable of these short trips was driving all the way to Washington, DC, some four hundred miles north, and climbing up every step of the Washington Monument. Occasionally, the family would go to a movie in Charlotte. For very special, quick getaways they would go for a couple of days to the Outer Banks in North Carolina on the Atlantic Ocean, or to Myrtle Beach, South Carolina, which was not yet the big tourist town that it is now.

The family lived a comfortable life, though like all Americans they were victims of the Great Depression, which began in late 1929. On the farm, however, the impact of economic downturn was felt less than it was by many people in other places. The cows on the farm still provided milk and cheese, and the farm's other crops still fed the family and workers. But Billy said that his father's money in the bank, which totaled $4,000, a large amount at that time, was totally lost. The hard work, which was their trademark as a family, would have to continue in order to rebuild, as was the case of so many Americans, and start over.

Faith was an essential part of the young family's life, as it was for many Americans in the early twentieth century. Billy's dad was raised Methodist in an era when the Methodist revivals were still popular. He was converted to Christ and Christian faith in 1908 at a Methodist revival at the age of eighteen. Years later, Billy's dad took five-year-old

Billy to hear a famous preacher, Billy Sunday, who at that time was a traveling evangelist in America. Young Billy was more interested in the fact that Billy Sunday had been a major league baseball player than he was in his passionate faith or the message that he preached that day.

Billy's mother, Morrow, was Scottish Presbyterian. Morrow had the more fervent faith of Billy's two parents by the time all the children came along. She taught Billy the Westminster Shorter Catechism when he was a boy.[7] Every Sunday, and I mean *every* Sunday, the family attended the Associate Reformed Presbyterian Church in downtown Charlotte. Billy's mother also made sure her husband and family practiced regular family devotions.

As Billy grew into adolescence he added two other loves to his life: cars and girls. He started driving the farm truck, a GMC, when he was eight. The farm foreman, Reese Brown, taught him to drive, and many other things as well. Reese was one of his father's best friends as well as his foreman. He'd been a sergeant in the First World War and was a highly gifted man and leader. Reese never hesitated to correct Billy Frank (Frank is Billy Graham's middle name) when he needed it, and Billy respected him very much. Reese was also an African American. For a farm in the South to have a black foreman who was best friends with the white owner was rare indeed. The presence of Reese Brown in Billy's life from an early age may have contributed to Graham's progressive views on civil rights in the 1950s and '60s. Graham was, after all, a child of the South. His grandfathers had been in the Confederacy. Yet when civil rights and systemic racism became the major narrative of American life, he was ahead of most of his peers in believing in equal rights for all, regardless of race. We will discuss this topic more fully in the chapter on racial justice later in the book.

By the time Billy was in high school, he had graduated from the farm truck to his father's Model T and was prone to speed and adventure, which would at times get him into trouble. As for girls, adolescent hormones emerged, and Billy had several girlfriends and enjoyed holding hands and kissing a lot. If the reader wants to know more about this aspect of his teen years, read his official autobiography, *Just as I Am*, and get it from, shall we say, "the horse's mouth." In *Just as I Am*, Billy speaks of a time during his senior year of high school when, after an evening rehearsal of the school play, one of the girls coaxed him into a dark classroom and begged him to make love to her. He attributes a prayer to God for help to enable him to say no, and then he ran away from the encounter. His upbringing and the values of the day in small-town America had already forged the commitment that he would not have sex until marriage, and he didn't.[8]

He continued playing baseball and was involved in other high school activities and his church youth group. He still milked his twenty cows every morning, rising at 2:30 AM, which when added to evening activities at school and church meant he only had three to five hours of sleep at night. He believed that such little sleep contributed to his grades averaging only a C in high school. As for his faith, it had never been strong up until that point in his life. If anything, it was more of a moral guide for him; and, of course, participation in church life was not something he chose for himself throughout his school years. It was required of him by his parents. I share this because in many religious homes, the faith of the children is not as personal and passionate as that of the parents. Every Christian parent longs for their children's faith to exceed their own. But each child must "own" their own faith.

I started this chapter by suggesting the "stunning regularity" of Billy Graham's boyhood. Many of his early experiences, and his milieu, are a representation of Americana at its imagined best. It might as well have been a scene in a Norman Rockwell painting, complete with apple pie cooling in the kitchen window. Or an episode of my beloved *Lassie*.

Nothing in the story so far suggests that this boy Billy Graham would become one of the most well-known people of twentieth- and twenty-first-century America, and throughout the world, for that matter. Sure, he came from a good family. His parents never divorced. He was surrounded by love and nurture. But in those generations many people had such solid upbringings. On the other hand, to many readers his background seems anything but normal. We live in a world in which many families are broken; morals are up for grabs; and relativism, pluralism, and the diaspora of ideas due to globalization have diluted accepted religious and social values. Civility seems to have been lost, and to many the concept of the "American Dream" is a joke. To you who are nodding your heads as you read this, I can see how you might see his childhood as quite extraordinary. Perhaps compared to today's social climate he started with a leg up. Normal for his day or abnormal when contrasted to ours: feel free to choose how you see Billy Graham's childhood.

Either way, however, two closing thoughts come to mind. First, the regularity of Billy's upbringing would help him relate to regular people everywhere once he started preaching. He didn't come from a very wealthy family. His was a true blue-collar upbringing. He'd learned firsthand the value and absolute necessity of hard work. He also liked the things most of us liked at his age. His grades weren't extraordinary. He never attended an elite school. He grew up in a nation of abject poverty, during the Great Depression, and in a region of our country where racism was tangible and sometimes violently real. Many would argue that it is real everywhere in our country even today. To sum up, he would be able to relate to "regular folk" like me and you both personally and culturally. His brother-in-law Leighton Ford told me that once the great American theologian Reinhold Niebuhr remarked that Billy Graham was "God's messenger to the little guy." I'm not sure Niebuhr meant that as a compliment, but it was. God loves us little guys.

My second thought in conclusion about Billy's early life and experiences is really more of a question. Why, when he wasn't a very passionate Christian as a boy, would he become one as an adult? What turned him into an on-fire religious young man? Also, why would God choose him, a very normal person, for a destiny he could not ever in his wildest imagination have imagined? Well, the answer to those related questions is in our next chapter. But before we go there, think about this: If God selected Billy Graham, a regular man who, as he was the first to say, was also very flawed, for a special vocation, then maybe, just maybe, he loves me and you and has a plan for our lives to make a difference in the world as well.

I like the verses in the Bible that say God made us all in his own image and likeness (Gen. 1:27–28). These verses suggest that we are each special. The Bible also tells us that God created each of us unique. He even knew us even before we were born (Ps. 139:13–18). Again, that argues for us being precious. Finally, the Bible says we are loved by God. Maybe you've heard this verse, "God so loved the world" (John

3:16). That includes you and me. We are made in his image, we are each unique, and we are each loved despite our flaws and brokenness. Let's hear it for normal flawed people who nevertheless are marvelously created and loved by God.

Even in recent years, I think that Billy thought about these things a lot. When I was with him and his evangelism team for the San Diego Festival in the summer of 2003, I watched Billy greet thousands of kids on a Saturday night, which was planned as an evening for the youth. By this time, he was a grandfather or great-grandfather in age compared to almost everyone present. He walked slowly out to the podium, paused, and then just looked all around the stadium as a standing ovation from the youth greeted him. The great jumbo screens allowed every one of the tens of thousands of people there to feel he was looking at them. Then, Billy spoke three words: "God loves you." He paused and turned to another part of the audience and said, "God loves you." I think he said those three words three or four more times. It was as if he was experiencing again for himself how much God loved him; and if God loved him, he loved every other regular, normal, unique, and also very flawed person in the world. And on that night, he especially wanted thousands of kids to know it as well. It was a holy and wonderful evening as several hundred came forward to link their young lives with the loving God of the universe.

I'll close this chapter with a verse that puts it all together for me and, I hope, will for you. "But God showed his great love for us by sending Christ to die for us while we were still sinners" (Rom. 5:8 NLT).

THREE

THE TIPPING POINT

*I tell you the truth, unless you are born again,
you cannot see the Kingdom of God.*
—John 3:3 (NLT)

———

And then it happened, sometime around my
sixteenth birthday. . . . I responded. I walked down
front as if I had lead weights attached to my feet
and stood in front of the platform. . . . I believe
that was the moment I made my real commitment
to Jesus Christ.

—BILLY GRAHAM[9]

How did Billy Graham "get religion"? How did he change from merely doing Christian religious activities to being consumed in his mind and heart with Jesus Christ? These are the questions we will consider in this chapter.

You might say it started in an almost fairy-tale sort of way, though this is a true tale. "Once upon a time," in May of 1934, a group of men from Charlotte, North Carolina, met in the fields of a farm outside of town for prayer. It was the farm of William Franklin Graham, Billy's father. While the men prayed in the field, the wives joined Morrow Graham, William's wife, to pray in the farmhouse. The prayer meeting was the fourth such gathering in the last eighteen months. The meetings were called for a special purpose. There was a sense that Charlotte needed a revival of living religion. Though the city was full of people who attended church, it was, to these praying men and women, devoid of true passion for God that leads to transformed lives.

Remember, the Great Depression was in full force during this time, and surely dire circumstances in people's everyday lives accelerated their sense of needing God to bring renewal. One of the men in attendance at this fourth meeting, according to Billy's father, prayed that the Lord would raise up someone to preach the gospel to the ends of the earth.[10] The reader might be thinking, "Okay, this must be where Billy Graham comes into the picture?" Well, yes it is, but not in the way you might think.

Billy remembered the prayer meeting. He had just come home from school and was at his chores pitching hay when he heard singing coming from the fields. One of the hired hands asked what the noise was all about. Billy told him, "I guess they're some fanatics that have talked Daddy into using the place."[11] In his autobiography, he comments that at this time he went to church weekly but grudgingly because he was forced to do so by his parents. Well, of course, these were not fanatics on Billy's daddy's farm, but earnest and sincere Christians doing the work of God that Billy would himself come to do one day.

The prayer meetings on the Graham farm led to an effort to host an evangelist to preach a revival in town. The great Billy Sunday himself had been there only ten years earlier. But this time the call went out to Mordecai Ham from Louisville, Kentucky. Like Billy Sunday and others before him, Reverend Ham would bring his own song leader and a comprehensive plan for awakening the city. He came in the fall of 1934 for twelve weeks of revival meetings. Billy remarked at the time that he would never go to hear the man. He said he wanted nothing to do with anyone called an evangelist. For the first month, Billy kept that vow, but Mordecai Ham was not your "normal" evangelist.

The Reverend Ham was deeply steeped in the Scriptures,[12] and took the time to study the city he was about to enter. He would start verbal fights with the powerful of a city including business leaders, government officials, educators, and especially the media regarding issues and actions he perceived as wrong and against God's desires. Each night he would point out sins of the city and region in which he was speaking. He understood that sin was not only personal but also societal, and he made it clear that a just God would judge not only people for their sins but also places where sin was revealed. The verbal sparring usually ended with newspapers challenging his premises. In this way, very soon the citizens of the city of a Ham revival would start attending the meetings, if only to hear what the fighting evangelist would say. We must remember that there was no television or modern forms of social media other than newspapers, print magazines, and radio, which still in its infancy. One can imagine, then, why so many would be drawn to the meetings.

Word got back to the soon-to-be sixteen-year-old Billy Graham about the evangelist's ability to take and throw verbal punches with the best of them. Billy is purported to have said to a friend who invited him to one of the meetings, "Is he a fighter? I like a fighter."[13] Then a story broke that a home across the street from one of the city's high schools had become a place of immoral activity during lunch times, with students gathering to do more than eat their lunches. Ham was relentless in his criticism of the school and the students. When Billy heard this news he decided to go to one of the meetings to hear from the evangelist for himself.

Billy said that he was spellbound by the preacher Ham on the very first night. His use of the Scriptures to discuss everyday realities caught his attention, and the emotion and energy of the meetings where upwards of five thousand people were attending each night brought more people to one place than Billy had ever seen. The comparatively staid Presbyterian church experiences that Billy had had up to that time didn't remotely approach the energy and passion of Mordecai's meetings, which were held in a freshly built wood and steel building. Sawdust was strewn across the ground to serve as the floor. If you've ever heard the phrase, "the sawdust trail," it was from these tabernacles constructed for revivals and then donated to the city when the event was over. During this era, tens of thousands of people would walk forward on the sawdust trail to confess their sins and commit their lives to Jesus Christ throughout every corner of America. The promise was that the love of God in Christ was sufficient to forgive confessing sinners for all their sins. This love was demonstrated by Jesus who died on a criminal's cross for the forgiveness of sins. This same message is given today in millions of churches and by the hundreds of millions of Christians who believe in this Good News of Jesus Christ.

After his first visit, Billy returned nearly every night for the final two months of the revivals. He heard messages on topics not often addressed in his church, such as heaven and hell, and God's moral requirements for people. It may have been that his church had clearly spoken on all these issues, but Billy was being drawn toward God, and the words of the Bible and the preacher began to convict him of his sin. He couldn't understand what was happening to him because he'd always thought of himself as a pretty good kid. He went to church regularly, was baptized and confirmed. He honored his parents and worked hard at his chores. And yet, something inside him said that his goodness was not good enough.

For those readers who've had the experience of the new birth that occurs when one confesses not their goodness, but their lack of it, you may recall how something deep inside you was pointing out how far away you were from God's righteous requirements for living. This was happening to young Billy Graham. He said that on some nights he was sure Mordecai Ham was speaking directly to him, and when he pointed to the audience Billy often felt that Ham was pointing directly at him. One night, in fact, Billy says that he sat purposely behind a woman with a big hat, so the evangelist couldn't point at him.[14]

During those two months of attending the revival meetings, Billy met other high school kids and became friends with two young men who would be with him the rest of his life: Grady and T. W. Wilson. Grady, especially, was also being drawn toward Jesus and suffered from the same sense of guilt for his past wrongs as Billy. The two of them actually joined the revival choir so that they could stand behind the evangelist with song books in front of their faces. Thus they would not fall victim to Reverend Ham's "accusatory stare"! Neither Grady nor Billy was naturally gifted for singing; in fact, much later, Billy's great soloist George Beverly Shea would kiddingly say of Billy, "He has a malady with the melody." Reverend Ham was probably never staring at them, but when God's Spirit begins to draw a person toward himself there is often an increasing sense of guilt over our shortcomings. Why? Because God points out the truth of our lives as he sees it from his state and standard of perfection. This enables us to see our need for his forgiveness and properly appreciate the love of God that washes away our sins through the sacrifice of his own perfect life in our place. Both Billy and Grady were in such a condition, and apparently it was getting worse as the revival continued. Billy realized he was unable to make himself better no matter how great his resolve.

Another reality was dawning on Billy as well. He said, "What was dawning on me during those weeks was the miserable realization that I did not know Jesus Christ for myself."[15] Billy didn't have a personal relationship with God. He knew a lot *about* God, but he didn't necessarily know and love God as one would a friend. He watched the hundreds of people going forward at the revival. They were passionate in their desires to know God. He wasn't. This troubled him. He knew that all his religious activities as a boy made him restless and resentful more than desiring of God. Something was very wrong.

In my own story of coming to faith in Jesus Christ, it was this issue that bothered me as well. With little church and religious background, I didn't even know a person could have a loving personal relationship with God. I am grateful for my Young Life leader and friends who first told me that I could have such a relationship. It was kind of an aching loneliness for a loving, faithful relationship that first drew me to God.

Billy's distressed soul was being hit on two sides. First, he had increasing guilt about his own sin. Second, he had an increasing desire to know God personally. The remedy for both was at hand. Then, on November 1, 1934, "around my sixteenth birthday," as Billy puts it in *Just as I Am*, after Reverend Ham finished his rampage on sin, he began to speak about God's love, using Romans 5:8 as his text: "But God demonstrates his own love for us in this: While we were still sinners, Christ died for us."[16] This was Billy's tipping point. When the evangelist gave the summons for people looking for God to come forward, Billy responded. He said he felt like he had lead weights attached to his feet as he walked the sawdust trail with three or four hundred others that evening. Many were weeping as they walked. Billy wasn't. No bells were going off. He felt no special emotion, yet he kept walking. Then a Christian friend of the family who saw him going forward stepped up, wrapped Billy in his arms, and helped him make his commitment to Jesus Christ. Billy's father came to him at the front of the hall too, and said how glad he was that Billy was taking his stand.

Later that evening, Billy remembers how he knelt at his bed of his own volition, not at his parents' insistence, and thanked God that something had happened to him that night. In the days and weeks that followed he knew he'd been truly converted because he found church meetings and activities to suddenly be interesting. The sermons became so compelling he started taking notes. Even the choir sounded better. He wanted to read and learn the Bible, and he found himself singing hymns to his cows. With a voice like his it was probably a miracle the cows kept producing milk!

Billy Graham is an example of someone who had Christian background and practices but had not experienced what the Bible calls the "new birth" until that November night in 1934. In our culture today, a Christian polling research firm has determined that nearly 50 percent of our current population is just like Billy was. Half of those, about 25 percent of Americans, say they are Christians because they live in America and have some Christian background. They don't necessarily practice Christian faith in any way, but they say they are Christians because of their heritage. We often categorize them as "cultural Christians." The other 25 percent are what some have called "casual Christians." Casual Christians may seldom attend church, or they may attend all the time. The key to their being "casual" is they seek to live moral lives following the Ten Commandments and other virtues as much as they are able, and probably consider themselves pretty good people, at least compared to others. They also believe their level of goodness is enough to be approved by God. Almost all culturals and casuals believe that if they died they would go to heaven because of their perceived degree of goodness.

Billy was a casual Christian before his tipping point—which is why he would very soon be willing to give his life to help the culturals and casuals see that they aren't really Christians at all until they enter a personal relationship with Jesus Christ. They have to repent of their sins and receive forgiveness. They need to have a personal relationship with God. A true Christian is a person who never believes they are good enough to please a holy God, but that God is good enough, perfect in fact, and will forgive all who believe and put their trust in him. The survey I referred to calls this group the "committed," and this group, too, constitutes about 25 percent of our population. What about the final 25 percent of Americans in that survey? They are what I might call the "closed." These are people who don't believe in Jesus Christ and his message and for the time being don't want to. They may be persons of other world religions or secularists who feel they don't need God. Or they may be angry at God for the injustices and sufferings of life and decide to forget about God altogether.[17]

In closing this chapter, I want to offer an appeal to any reader who would say, "I am a 'cultural' or 'casual' Christian, or I am at present 'closed' to Christianity." Billy Graham would tell you that God loves you, but also that you are in everlasting danger if you don't receive

God's love through a personal relationship with Jesus Christ. Why everlasting danger? Because people who want little or nothing to do with God in this life cannot expect God to force a person to be with him in heaven. Why would he do such a thing? It violates his love to force you to love him and be with him.

Billy would tell you that by knowing Christ personally you receive an abundant life on earth and eternal life with him in heaven. Dear readers, please consider Christ. Do you sense him drawing you toward him right now? If so humbly say something like this:

> Dear God, I need you. Forgive me for all my sins and especially for choosing to lead my own life. Thank you that Jesus Christ, your Son, loved me so much he died in my place. I commit my life to you today.

If you have prayed that prayer, or something similar to it, then today may be your tipping point. Please look in the back of the book right now to help you with your next steps. Chapter 10 will be important for you. God bless you.

FOUR

PREPARING FOR HIS FUTURE

*Jesus grew in wisdom and in stature and in favor
with God and all the people.*
—Luke 2:52 (NLT)

———

To be a disciple is to be committed to Jesus Christ
as Savior and Lord and committed to follow him
every day. To be a disciple is also to be disciplined
in our bodies, minds, and souls.

—BILLY GRAHAM[18]

Billy Graham was born again. A new, vibrant relationship with God replaced his previous dissatisfying religious life. In that previous life, he practiced the dictates of the Christian faith as he'd been taught. But there was no passion and very little love for God in them. Now he found himself loving God and wanting to practice the dictates of his faith. Neither Billy nor anyone in his family thought his conversion meant he'd become a minister or pastor, much less an evangelist to the world.

He graduated from high school in the spring of 1936. A friend, Albert McMakin, who first invited him to hear Mordecai Ham, now invited him to join the Fuller Brush Company, where he worked and sold brushes during the summer. This would be a good way to earn some money for college in the fall. His friends Grady and T. W. Wilson joined him as well. Billy went door to door and soon learned how to honestly offer quality brushes to housewives. He also learned to ask God for help in his work. He would pray for each household he would visit, and not only to sell brushes to them but for opportunities to talk with them about spiritual things.[19] It shouldn't surprise us that often he had a chance to tell someone on his daily route about Jesus Christ. As the summer came to a close, it was time to head to college. For the next six years, he would pursue formal education, though like many young people even today, he was not sure what he'd be doing when he was done.

For young Billy, Bob Jones College proved to be a mixture of good and difficult. It was in the fall of 1936 when Billy's father drove Billy and the Wilson brothers across the Appalachians to Cleveland, Tennessee, the home of Bob Jones College. Christian evangelist Bob Jones Sr. had founded the school less than a decade earlier, in Florida, but after a disastrous hurricane, followed by financial struggles during the Great Depression, he moved the college to east Tennessee in 1933. Reverend Jones had spoken at the boys' high school in Charlotte and had made quite an impression. This would be the beginning of Billy's formal education. Bob Jones College specialized in teaching the Bible—Jones founded the school in response to what he saw as rising secularism in American life—but also taught the value of the liberal arts.

Billy learned two important things at Bob Jones College. The first lesson came from listening to Bob Jones preach evangelistically. Billy discovered that the call to be an evangelist was indeed a high calling for any young man. His own heart began to be gripped by a passion for souls and humankind's desperate need for Christ.[20] He wondered if he might not be called by God to such a future. Second, Billy appreciated the college's view of the arts. Music, literature, and theatrical arts were valued, something quite surprising for a "fundamentalist" school that held suspect anything in culture not explicitly endorsed by Scripture. Jones Sr.'s own son, Bob Jones Jr. (who would become the school's president in 1947 and move it to Greenville, South Carolina), was an accomplished Shakespearean actor. In that fall semester, the school put on *Macbeth*, and Billy had a minor role.

But there was a flip side to Bob Jones College that Graham and his friends found difficult to swallow. The rules in the school at that time were debilitating and discouraging. It seemed there were rules about everything, including even a command to snitch on others who were not following the rigid requirements. Billy said that students were watched as if by hawks from above.[21] In addition to this, the intellectual climate was oppressive. There was little openness to questions from students interacting with the curriculum, trying to make sense out of their faith. Billy was a life-embracing young man with tremendous curiosity. The climate of controlled learning wasn't conducive to his nature.

There were other difficulties as well. During that first fall semester, he got sick with the flu, which one author suggests may have led to melancholy feelings or a sort of mild depression.[22] In a meeting with Dr. Jones at the time, Billy confessed his discontent and his thoughts of leaving the school. Dr. Jones, Billy said, "pronounced me a failure and predicted only more failure ahead. I left his office disillusioned and dejected."[23] The final straw for the young Graham came when he and a friend were disciplined for leaving campus without proper permission. They had left to preach at a local church.

When he came home from Bob Jones College for Christmas break, Billy knew he didn't want to return. He had confided in his parents about his struggles during the semester. His mother had counseled him to understand that God allows testing and afflictions to strengthen our faith. She told him that he would soon sense the touch of God.[24] Her words helped, but he was to struggle deeply for several more weeks.

I sat down recently with Billy's sister Jeanie, who was just four when Billy was a freshman at Bob Jones. Jeanie remembers the night Billy and his father came in the house at about midnight upon his returning home from school.[25] Billy was her big brother (he the oldest and she the youngest of the siblings). They had always been close and happy together. In fact, she recalls a time when he had put her on his tall shoulders and went racing through the house for a ride. What he didn't take into proper account was how tall he was and how short entryways could be. Jeanie's head hit the entryway and she went flailing onto the floor. She wasn't badly hurt, however. What she remembers from that event and many others is her happy-go-lucky and caring big brother.

On that first night when Billy and his dad arrived at home late from Bob Jones, Jeanie remembers Billy gently entering her room to awaken and embrace his sleeping little sister. Could it be that he needed her that night to be his little sis, the one who would let him back into the place where he was allowed and encouraged to be an imperfect but curious and energetic young man, who perhaps understood that he loved God and was simply searching for what it means to be an adult?

In the Winnie-the-Pooh tales at the end of *The House at Pooh Corner*, Christopher Robin realizes he's growing up and that soon he'll not be allowed to do "nothing" anymore. When Pooh inquires why, Christopher Robin simply says, "They don't let you." The strict requirements of Bob Jones College in many ways was a "they don't let you" experience for a free-spirited young man. Now that he was home, Jeanie and the family would be used by God to replace his melancholy with hope and joy. Indeed, his parents had the spark of an idea about a school that might better fit their eldest son.

Mrs. Graham had read of Florida Bible Institute (FBI) in a *Moody Monthly* magazine. Billy had also heard about the place from his friend Wendell Phillips, who had left Bob Jones College and already chosen FBI as his new place to learn. The school was founded in Hillsborough County, near Tampa, by another traveling evangelist, Dr. William T. Watson, in 1932. Since the Graham family had already planned to go to Florida for the Christmas holidays, they decided that they should see it for themselves.

Billy liked the palm trees, the abundant orange orchards, and certainly the warmer climate. And after that family visit, he was determined and encouraged by his parents to go ahead and withdraw from Bob Jones in order to attend FBI. Billy arrived for the beginning of the spring semester in late January 1937. Sister Jeanie still remembers that initial visit to the Florida campus, when the family was vacationing with relatives for Christmas. In his autobiography, Billy says that at one point his daddy lifted little Jean onto a table, and she began to preach. He writes, "She was so cute, with her beautiful blond hair, that they stopped to pay attention."[26] Jeanie told me she still remembers what she said that day, namely, "If you don't believe in Jesus, you are going straight to hell."[27] But there is a twist to this story: Jean remembers that it was Billy, not her daddy, who set her on the table and told her to preach. If this is accurate, then we can say Billy encouraged his sister to be an evangelist before he became one!

The Florida Bible Institute was housed in a large, abandoned resort that included a golf course and a hotel capable of lodging at least fifty guests. The Temple Terrace Resort and Country Club had closed during the Great Depression, making the land available to Dr. Watson at a rock-bottom price. He saw it as a great location for a Bible school. It was the color of pink flamingos, and large enough to provide lodging for the students as well as guests who came to Florida to vacation in a warmer climate. The guests would often be pastors and missionaries from colder climates who came to relax and play golf, and often preach in the chapel, as well as function as guest teachers in some of the courses taught throughout the curriculum. Some of the guests were, in fact, famous preachers of the day. The resulting atmosphere for learning, both in the classroom and all over campus, was electric and eclectic. Forty women and thirty men were enrolled when Billy began his first semester, representing a wide range of Christian denominations from all over the United States. Billy enjoyed his newfound freedom to explore and learn, as well as the Florida sunshine. This all suited young Graham perfectly.

Billy soon became an insatiable learner. His sister remembers him as a teenage boy reading for hours on end. He would lie on the floor in the living room of the farmhouse, devouring books. He loved history, biographies of leaders, and adventure stories. Florida Bible Institute fed this sense of discovery in books, and Billy became interested, even then, in politics and events happening at home and abroad. He also began to love learning about the Christian faith in all its dimensions. His brother-in-law Leighton Ford, Jeanie's husband, was once asked what was unique about Billy Graham. He responded that Billy was a lifelong learner.[28] Even in later years, Graham's intellectual curiosity was unabated. Dr. David Bruce, who manages Billy's offices today in Montreat, North Carolina, remembers fondly Billy reading the latest biographies on American leaders such as John Adams, and famous Christian leaders including Dietrich Bonhoeffer. He was, David says, always asking Christian leaders what he needed to be reading to keep up with ideas especially in theology, missions, and evangelism.

I recall visiting Billy at the Tampa Crusade in 2001. He asked me and the provost of Wheaton College, Stanton Jones, what kinds of trends were happening in evangelism that he should know about. He was eighty-three years old at the time! This was also as he was about to go upstairs onto a vast football field and preach to tens of thousands of people. He wanted to hear about anything we had to say before he did so. In his last years, he was unable to read because of his failing eyesight. And, because his hearing was very bad, it was difficult for him to dialogue with people about intellectual matters. I can only imagine how difficult that would have been for a man who simply loved to learn.

In 1937, at the age of nineteen, his mind and energies were kindled by all the Florida Institute had to offer. The students worked part-time jobs at the institute as a way of keeping tuition affordable. They cleaned rooms, served guests in the dining hall, and even caddied on the golf course. Through these interactions they learned about Christian leadership by watching, listening, and talking with the many notable luminaries. The classroom and the interaction provided two of the means for learning. The third was the institute's hands-on learning by "doing" gospel work in the greater Tampa community. Teams of students were sent out wherever there was a need or an opportunity to proclaim Christ. They visited churches, missions, trailer parks, and prisons. Sometimes they stood on street corners and tried to draw crowds to listen.

On one occasion, the dean of the institute, Dr. John Minder, invited Billy to join him for a Sunday-night service at a local Baptist church. Minder had been asked to preach. On the Saturday preceding the meeting, while visiting with the church pastor, Dr. Minder turned the tables on Billy. Rather than watching Minder preach, Billy would preach, he told the church pastor. This would be his first formal message in a local church. Billy responded, "I've never preached a formal sermon in front of a church audience."[29] Evidently, both men laughed at him and said they would pray for him. Billy spent almost the entire night in prayer and preparation. He'd gathered four borrowed sermons that he'd adapted and practiced but never preached live. He was known to have often rowed out to a small island in the little lake next to the institute in order to preach to the birds, alligators, and insects, but this would be to real people. Billy practiced all day on Sunday and, as the story goes, chose one of the four sermons to preach, hoping to fill twenty or thirty minutes. That evening forty or so people were in the congregation, including the song leader, who was chewing tobacco, and farmers, ranchers, and their wives. Billy was exceedingly nervous, and his knees were knocking when he stood up to preach. When he finished his first sermon, he felt it had concluded too quickly, so he went on to the second sermon he knew, and then on to the third, then the fourth. Finally, he sat down. Eight minutes had passed.[30]

Billy's first preaching experience in front of a real congregation was by no means illustrious, but the occasion would lead to crafting many others while he studied in Florida for those three years. His hard work, prayer, and practice showed fruit. Before he graduated he was guest preacher at many leading churches and had a regular speaking assignment at a trailer park that drew hundreds of people. Minder asked him to be his replacement pastor and preacher for a summer at the large Tampa Gospel Tabernacle. There he learned to preach to the same congregation regularly and perform the many duties required of a pastor. Billy's respect for the pastoral office has always been high. Perhaps it was that summer that gave him such respect for the office.

Soon, Billy began to wonder if his life calling was to be a preacher. One night he went out on the golf course and lay prostrate on the edge of one of the greens. He was deeply moved and wept as he prayed, "Oh God, if you want me to serve you, I will."[31] His will was now yielded to receive a clear calling from God to the ministry. However, the unique call to be an evangelist was still ahead.

Two other notable events occurred while he was in Florida. While his love of baseball and dream of being a major league ballplayer began to wane in Florida, his love of girls did not. Very early on, he met a fellow student who was a singer and hoped to become a missionary following graduation. Her name was Emily Cavanaugh. Billy was smitten with her. She liked him too, drawn not only to his good looks but also to his charisma, energy, and passion for people. He actually proposed to Emily by letter during the summer break of his first year at the institute. Emily liked him but felt uncomfortable with the speed of the relationship. She needed more time. Months later, she told him she was warming to the idea of marrying him. Evidently, he took that as a yes, while to Emily it was still a maybe. In May of 1938, nearly a year after he asked her to marry him, she told him at the end of the annual institute spring banquet that it would be better if they didn't date for a while. Billy was heartbroken. He went to Dr. Minder that night and poured out his sadness. The dean stayed up with the nineteen-year-old almost the whole night. The pain was deep and ongoing. At that time, Billy wrote to his friend Wendell Phillips, "All the stars have fallen out of my sky. There is nothing to live for. We have broken up."[32]

But a new introspection came upon Billy at that time. He would take long nighttime walks on the golf course wondering why this had happened and what he should now do with his life. On one of these moonlit strolls on the course, Billy had been arguing with the Lord. "I can't preach, I don't want to preach. No church would have me." But the Lord, he said, "talked right back. 'I can use you, I need you. You make the choice and I will find the place.'"[33] On the eighteenth green he knelt, and then lying prostrate on the golf course, he said, "Lord, I'll go wherever you want me to go, and I'll preach wherever you want me to preach."[34]

Emily Cavanaugh ended up marrying another boy from the Florida Bible Institute named Charles Massey, who became a very successful pastor himself. The Masseys, in fact, would become good friends to Billy and Ruth Graham in the years to come. Ruth had a secret hope that when meeting Emily for the first time she would be a plain-looking woman. In reality, Ruth said, "She was drop dead gorgeous."[35]

Billy would be true to his commitment to God on the golf course. Later, he wrote another letter to Wendell. In it he said, "I have settled it once and for all with the Lord. No girl or friend or anything shall ever come first in my life. I have resolved that the Lord Jesus Christ shall have all of me. I care not what the future holds. I have determined to follow Him at any cost."[36]

The cost would be higher than he could imagine as a nineteen-year-old. But he'd hold true to it. He would in future years be tempted to follow other paths, but as we'll see, he would stay true. His formal and informal education ended at Florida Bible Institute in May of 1940. The Second World War had descended on Europe. Billy followed events through newspapers and the radio. Before he was converted, he'd heard Adolf Hitler on the radio in his dad's car. He later wrote, "I was particularly fascinated by the oratorical style of his speeches shouted in an almost hypnotic voice. . . . He frightened me in some way, even though I did not understand his language."[37] Little did he know then how the same man would frighten the whole world and show even more clearly why Christ was the only answer to the human and natural disasters of our world.

Billy's graduation service at Florida Bible took place on May 13, 1940. On the very same day, Winston Churchill, the new prime minister of the British Empire, delivered his famous speech about never surrendering to Hitler's regime, but that it would require blood, toil, tears, and sweat to do so. Another speech was given that day at Florida Bible Institute, by the valedictorian, Vera Resue. It is worth reading some of her words in light of this moment in Billy's life and the world at large:

The early church faced darkness as Rome began to take complete control. It seemed as though the light was near extinction, but God was waiting for someone who would dare to accept the challenge. Martin Luther was that one. He heard the Voice of God and in the face of opposition from every side, he stepped forth from the darkness bearing the True Light, "the light that lighteth up the world." Again we see dawn; but as we delve back in the history of the Christian church we find that these conditions existed time and again. Each time God had a chosen human instrument to shine forth His Light in the darkness. Men like Luther, John and Charles Wesley, Moody and others were ordinary men, but men who heard the Voice of God. Their surrounding conditions were as black as night, but they had God. "If God be with us who can be against us?" It has been said that Luther revolutionized the world. It was not he, but Christ working through him. The time is ripe for another Luther, Wesley, Moody. There is room for another name in this list. There is a challenge facing us.[38]

Every one of those graduates would probably contribute to facing the global challenges of their generation and extending the kingdom of God to the world. One of them, however, unbeknownst to anyone present that day in Temple Terrace, Florida, would soon be counted by many as the next name on that list.

God had one more stop for Billy Graham in his formal education. He had been a student at Bob Jones College for one semester. He had studied at Florida Bible Institute for three and a half years and graduated. While there he'd met a couple of guests at the hotel who had affiliation with a Christian liberal arts college in the North by the name of Wheaton. They encouraged Billy to round out his education with a liberal arts degree and argued that Wheaton College was excellent and up to the task. They helped him get acceptance, and in the fall of 1940 Billy was headed to the Chicago suburbs. His whole life had been spent in the South, visiting Northern cities only on vacations, and once, in the summer of 1940, when he and a friend had held some small but effective evangelistic and revival meetings in York, Pennsylvania.

Not only was Wheaton in a Northern state, but it was also a nationally recognized school with a strong reputation for scholarly excellence. Students from all forty-eight states attended Wheaton, not to mention many missionary kids who'd been raised in other parts of the world. There were also African American students at Wheaton, something new for Billy in a classroom. The school was, in fact, founded in 1860 by pastor and abolitionist Jonathan Blanchard, who set out to build a faculty and curriculum grounded in the liberal arts and devoted to what were then radical social ideas. In recent years, documentation has been found to validate what had long been known, that Wheaton College in its earliest days was a stop for fleeing blacks on the Underground Railroad.[39] Billy's cultural understandings were about to expand.

He would in Wheaton find a liberal arts school as theologically grounded as Florida Bible Institute, with a strong commitment to evangelism of the lost, while at the same time devoted to all means of social improvement. The school was also a challenge by virtue of its size: it dwarfed the Florida Bible Institute. At that time, Wheaton had more than eleven hundred students. Billy's mind was firmly focused on his studies thanks to his rigorous education at the institute. And they needed to be, for Wheaton was a school of high academic reputation. In fact, given the academic rigors at Wheaton, little of Billy's course work transferred from Florida Bible Institute, so in many ways he was starting over. He entered Wheaton at almost twenty-two years of age and was only at the rank of a second-semester freshman. Nevertheless, Billy applied himself seriously to the task at hand, and by the end of his first year his grade average across all courses was a B+.

He was clearly up to the challenge academically, though for a time he felt culturally unsettled and lonely. This loneliness would not last long, as he soon began meeting students and faculty. In fact, on one of his first days the president of the school, Dr. Raymond Edman, greeted Billy by name. Dr. Edman's brother had been one of the businessmen in Florida who had told Billy about Wheaton.

Billy also got involved in the Wheaton Gospel Teams early in the term, allowing him to meet students of like heart and passion for ministry. Gospel Teams comprised a preacher and musicians. Nine teams would speak and sing in churches and missions throughout Chicagoland. While most of the churches were small, especially for the Sunday-night meetings, they were fervent in spirit. Billy was used to speaking to larger audiences after his experiences in Florida and the Southeast, and so he enjoyed serving and preaching on these teams. Soon, his reputation as a charismatic and gifted preacher became well known on campus. He was so effective that by the autumn of 1941, only one year after he came to Wheaton, President Edman asked him to take over his duties as pastor of the Gospel Tabernacle in downtown Wheaton. It met in a Masonic Lodge on Sundays and Wednesday nights and could hold three hundred people. Billy preached three times each week at the Tabernacle and performed other pastoral duties as well. This, again, probably helped him gain appreciation for the local church and the complex and never-ending duties of pastors.

A rumor has been circulating for decades that Billy Graham was a Mason. About ten years ago, I received a letter from someone who had heard me preach and wanted to know what degree of Masonry I held, since Billy Graham was also a Mason and I was now working with him. Billy Graham was not a Mason, and I am not either. However, Billy did use a Masons' building during those Wheaton years to hold an evangelical church. That's probably the reason the rumor emerged.

During his first year at Wheaton, Billy had another life-altering experience, when he met the young woman who was to become his wife. She had grown up in a missionary family in China, where her father was a medical doctor. Dr. and Mrs. Bell sent their daughter Ruth from China to Wheaton College. Ruth believed that, like her parents, she was called by God to be a missionary. She wanted to return to Asia and reach Tibet. She was also by all eyewitness accounts a beautiful young woman, with strong faith in Christ, rising at four in the morning to do her devotions.

A friend of Billy's told him about Ruth. When Billy first saw her, the story goes, he was absolutely smitten. He was also a bit cautious after his painful experience with Emily in Florida. Ruth and Billy's first date was to attend a performance of Handel's *Messiah* on campus. On the way back to her dorm, he tried to hold her hand, but she pulled it away. As a result, Billy assumed she was not interested. But that was not the case. Ruth was confused and attracted to Billy. But she felt she was called to the mission field in Tibet and was so dedicated to that calling that she assumed she would remain single her whole life. So, while Billy went back to his room saddened, Ruth got on her knees and prayed a now quite famous prayer: "God, if you let me serve You with that man, I'd consider it the greatest privilege of my life."[40]

For the next year, they would date and share campus life. Billy asked Ruth to marry him in the spring of 1941. She did want to marry him, but she was still committed to being a missionary in Tibet. Billy prayed as to whether the mission field was the call on his life too, although by this time he thought it was to be an evangelist, and primarily in America. Much praying and turmoil took place over the next months as their competing callings caused concern and much discussion between them. The situation was further exacerbated when Ruth's sister contracted tuberculosis the same spring that Billy proposed. Ruth dropped out of Wheaton in order to care for her in New Mexico until the following fall. Yet God was in charge of their relationship. Both the young man and young woman were fully devoted to God's will throughout the process. Even from a distance they communicated through letters. Little did they know that much of their lives they would communicate through letters, as Billy's travels would eventually take him all over the world.

On July 6, 1941, Billy received a thick envelope in the mail from Ruth. One of the first sentences read, "I'll marry you."[41] I can only imagine the sense of relief and gratitude he must have experienced at that moment! The many pages of the letter that followed explained how Ruth had become sure she was to marry Billy and to follow him wherever God would lead them together. They had still not had their first kiss. But many were soon to come!

Billy and Ruth would graduate from Wheaton College together in May of 1943. They would marry just two months later, on August 13, 1943, in Montreat, North Carolina, which in a matter of a few years would become the place of their lifelong home. When Ruth died in 2007, Billy said, "The song is gone from our home."[42] Until his death Billy resided in the home they made together for so many decades—a life that started at Wheaton College. I will share more about their marriage and the wonderful family God gave them in a later chapter.

Billy's preparation for his unique call came through formal education at two colleges and one Bible institute. Altogether he had seven years of post-high-school education, earning two bachelor's degrees (the FBI degree was an unaccredited bachelor of theology) in the process. But there was another dimension of his education that cannot be overlooked. Billy's period of preparation was linked to some special individuals. From these men and women he gained more than academic knowledge. From them he experienced what I would call "whole-life development."

There is a verse in the Gospel of Luke that speaks of Jesus's whole-life development: "And Jesus grew in wisdom and stature, and in favor with God and man" (Lk. 2:52). Jesus grew mentally, physically, spiritually, and socially, since he was fully human as well as divine. It is more than appropriate to imagine that God wishes all his children to grow in these ways as well. We don't know how Jesus grew in these four important ways, as the Scriptures don't provide many details, but we do know that when he began his three years of public ministry he immediately gathered twelve men around him and poured his life into them. Two church-growth consultants have recently written that Jesus spent about 75 percent of his time with the twelve and only 25 percent with the masses of people.[43] They were with Jesus all the time. They watched him interact with his family and his village. They walked with him throughout Israel in those years. They ate together, bedded down in inns, and slept on the ground. They watched him interact with individuals from all walks of life as he preached and taught crowds of people. His whole life was displayed in front of them, and they discussed with him all the issues he addressed while alive. They even watched him die. Finally, those original disciples were witnesses of his resurrected life for a period of forty days.

In today's vernacular we call this kind of whole-life education *mentoring*. Generally speaking, mentors are about a generation older than the recipient of their wisdom and experience. They may also sometimes be peers. Sometimes a mentor comes into a younger leader's life for only a season. Others might be involved for many seasons. Billy was blessed with both kinds. A mentor is someone who is "a brain to pick, a shoulder to cry on, and someone who kicks us in the pants when we need it."[44] A friend of mine, Dr. Leighton Ford, who has been an older mentor in my life for nearly thirty years, says that a mentor is a "friend on the journey, and an artist of the soul."[45]

Graham was deeply influenced by his mentors. For example, Dr. John Minder, the dean of Florida Bible Institute, played a vital role in Billy's whole-life development during those important late teens and very early twenties, a relationship that began when he met Billy and his father on their first visit to campus. Billy would come to call Dr.

Minder his "father in the ministry."[46] Minder was twenty years older than Billy. He was single and had lots of time to pour into younger leaders. He taught Billy in the classroom, took him with him on preaching assignments, and as we saw earlier, opened doors for his first preaching opportunity in a church. He counseled Billy when he had vocational decisions to make, and he was with him through the great sorrows with Emily Cavanaugh.[47]

Then, as we saw earlier, when Billy arrived at Wheaton College, he was greeted by name early on by President Edman. Perhaps Edman knew Billy was having a tough time adapting to a large school in the North nearly one thousand miles from his home. "Doc" Edman, as he was affectionately called by students, was known for being readily available to anyone in need. Still, Billy seems to have received some special attention because of his unique gifts and apparent calling. Edman counseled, advised, and guided Billy. When Edman handed over the preaching and leadership of Gospel Tabernacle to the much younger man, he'd only known Billy a year. Doc Edman would also guide Billy in his relationship with Ruth, giving his blessing to Billy and Ruth one day as they crossed paths on campus, telling Billy, "Bill, Ruth's one in a million."[48] Long after Billy left Wheaton College, President Edman would continue to provide needed wisdom and theological insight as the young evangelist's preaching career took off. He would travel often to be with Billy at crusades. He was a mentor in every sense of the word.

Mentors open doors of opportunity for younger leaders. Sometimes a mentor can see a preferred future for a younger leader that the leader cannot see. Torrey Johnson was another such mentor to Billy Graham following his graduation from Wheaton. Billy and

Ruth had accepted a call to pastor the Western Springs Baptist Church, not far from the college and also in the Chicago suburbs. One day Johnson, who pastored a leading church in the area and was about ten years older than Billy, was driving down a street as Billy was about to pass in the opposite direction. He pulled alongside Billy's car and introduced himself. Billy was excited to meet Torrey who, in addition to pastoring, was also broadcasting Christian content on the radio.[49] That introduction led to a series of meetings where Johnson offered Billy one of his radio programs because he couldn't pastor and handle two programs at the same time. The radio program, called *Songs in the Night*, was broadcast weekly on Sunday evenings before a live audience. It drew young people from throughout Chicagoland and especially returning war veterans. Billy was thrilled at the opportunity, and his church was willing to host the Sunday-evening event. Incidentally, Billy's church was quite small at that time, fewer than fifty people. Yet they supported their young pastor in his dreams. He needed a singer to help him and took a chance on asking a very popular Christian artist by the name of George Beverly Shea to partner with him. Bev, as he was called by friends throughout his long life, said yes. I have parishioners in my own congregation who are now in their eighties who used to attend *Songs in the Night* broadcasts from the Western Springs Church. They treasure the memories.

But Torrey Johnson had even more in mind for Billy and their witness for Christ. Torrey believed God was calling him to reach more and more young people for Christ, including returning servicemen, for these were the turbulent years of the Second World War when many young American boys were serving abroad and then coming back wounded in either body or spirit. In 1944, Torrey started a ministry called Chicagoland Youth for Christ, which used large rallies with entertainment, great music, and preaching to reach people for Jesus. He asked Billy to speak at their first event on May 27 of that year. Forty people came forward to commit their lives to Christ.[50] Before long, Youth for Christ rallies were occurring throughout the Midwest. Torrey's vision was to see it spread throughout the nation and internationally. During a fishing trip to Florida, he invited Billy to be the first full-time preaching evangelist for Youth for Christ. Billy left his pastorate in order to accept the role. Within a year, Youth for Christ was active in three hundred cities. Billy's calling to preach Christ for salvation was clear, and the impact of his preaching was great. His future was being forged by God through an older leader who saw in him what he didn't fully see in his life.

Minder, Edman, and Johnson were three sterling examples of mentoring in Graham's life. Many others would come along for a season, or seasons, to guide the young evangelist. Even as he aged and matured, he was fortunate to have such whole-life guides. A few of the many other names were Harold Ockenga, Dawson Trotman, Henrietta Mears, and Harold Pew, who may be known to some readers already. Each of them would play a key role in Billy's life.

Over time, Billy would pass on the mentoring ministry to others. Leighton Ford remembers helping to plan a Youth for Christ rally in his city. His mentor, Evan Hedley, had given him the assignment at the very early age of fourteen. But Leighton organized it and was able to secure the famous youth evangelist Billy Graham to come and speak. Leighton remembers the night as if it were yesterday. A crowd came and Graham preached, but only one person responded to the invitation. Leighton was dejected, something Billy may have recognized. Before he left the auditorium that night, Billy put his hand on Leighton's shoulder and said, "Leighton, I believe God has a calling on your life. If you stay humble, God will greatly use you."[51] A few years later, Billy would help Leighton get accepted at Wheaton College. He would also encourage Jeanie, his precious little sister, to think of Leighton as a "potential" life partner. According to Leighton, Billy suggested two young men to her and Leighton was one of them. Jeanie chose Leighton, and Billy became his brother-in-law. Billy would continue mentoring Leighton by opening doors for him as Billy's career soared. Soon, Leighton was an associate evangelist in the Graham organization, and over time he became a recognized Christian statesman throughout the evangelical world.

Many, many years later, Leighton and Jean Ford would sense that Leighton should step aside from speaking at large campaigns and leading ministry movements around the world and devote the remainder of his life to mentoring younger leaders. When he told Billy of his plan, Billy said, "Leighton, you're doing the right thing. I wish I'd done more in that regard."[52] Leighton began the work of mentoring at about age sixty. Scores have benefited, including me. Now, his mentoring principles are being practiced by hundreds, who have influenced thousands.

It's impossible to measure the impact informal mentoring education had on Billy Graham's life. Perhaps you, the reader, find yourself thinking about key individuals who have invested deeply in your own life. I certainly do, and I find myself wondering for who I am to be, to quote again one excellent definition of a mentor, a "shoulder to cry on, a brain to pick, and an encourager to help others see what they cannot see for themselves."

FIVE

INTIMATE GOD CONNECTION

One of those days Jesus went out to a mountainside to pray, and spent the night praying to God.
—Luke 6:12

———

The mightiest force in the world, as Frank Laubach called prayer, undergirded me and brought the blessing of God from Heaven to Los Angeles.

—BILLY GRAHAM[53]

O ne of Billy's close associates, Dr. Tom Phillips, was with him for a pastors' question-and-answer meeting in San Diego many years ago. One of the pastors present, Tom, asked Graham how he managed his daily personal relationship with God on days that were busy from morning to night with ministry duties. What did he do when he had to skip a day or two of personal devotional time? Phillips says that Billy quietly pondered the question. Then "he hemmed and hawed a bit as he tried to answer." Tom was surprised because Billy seemed always at his best in question-and-answer settings and was seldom at a loss for words. Finally, he spoke, and shyly said, "Well, I don't ever remember missing a day of personal time alone with God."[54]

I am often asked how Billy could remain so faithful to his calling for so long. I respond that it was because of his deep, abiding trust in and relationship with God. Billy's source of strength, both emotionally and physically, was his life with God. His relationship with God included God's speaking to him by his indwelling Spirit through intuition, and especially through the clarity that came through reading and studying the Bible. Someone has said that the Bible is God's love letter to his children. It is God's clear and direct language, and for those who practice reading it, it becomes a source for ongoing intimate dialogue. This is not to suggest that Graham treated his devotional life as a means to an end. He didn't do devotions because they provided wisdom and power. The wisdom and guidance were a by-product of daily quiet times. He practiced his devotional life because it nurtured his personal relationship with God. He loved God, he adored God, he worshiped God. He wanted to be as close to God as was humanly possible.

Being close to God is why Jesus spent so much time withdrawing from crowds and his disciples. He wanted "alone time" with God. Think about it. Jesus, the Son of God, became a human being for about thirty-three years. When he did that, he gave up for those earthly years the nearness of the everlasting and intimate connection enjoyed with God the Father from eternity. No wonder he slipped away whenever possible to connect with the Father in prayer and worship!

When a person experiences the new birth, and God's Spirit dwells within him or her, the desire to be with God becomes the strongest passion of life. This was true for Billy, and it can be true for all who are his adopted children through the new birth. If you, the reader, wonder if this is possible for you, I would say, "Yes it is!" You can become a friend of God by confessing your sins, and asking him to come into your life by his Holy Spirit. He longs for closeness with you, even more than you long for it yourself. Anyone who starts this journey will be forever grateful.

As for Billy, his boyhood friend and colleague for decades T. W. Wilson called him "the most completely disciplined person I have ever known."[55] Billy would start each day around 7:00 AM, when he would read five psalms and one chapter from the book of Proverbs. He started there because the Psalms helped him relate personally with God, while Proverbs provided principles on how to relate to people and the world.[56]

Not long before Billy's death, I asked Dr. David Bruce, the man who ran Graham's offices and oversaw his care, how or if Billy still had time each day with God. Here's what he said:

> During the last few years of his life, Mr. Graham has been robbed of his ability to read as a result of advancing Macular Degeneration. Consequently, it has been a few years since he was able to read his Bible and other devotional material.

David went on:

> When Mr. Graham realized that he could no longer participate in personal reading, he asked those on his staff—and eventually his nursing personnel who care for him—to begin and end each day with Bible reading and prayer. His devotional book of choice has been the iconic *Daily Light*—a

daily reading based on Scripture passages around a specific
theme. In these latter years, with the help of others around him,
[he] has not missed the opportunity of a daily devotional life.[57]

Tom Phillips remembers traveling with Billy to crusades and
being asked to come to Billy's hotel room almost daily to brief him
on events. He told me that Billy would have books and a few Bibles
open in different locations on his bed, the desk, even the chairs. He
was constantly working on his messages for each night, or on talks he
was giving during the day. But, Tom says, the many Bibles had another
reason as well. He watched Billy move throughout his hotel room and
pick up a Bible and read it for just a few moments. Then he might
move to another Bible and do the same. Why? Billy told Tom that he
liked to "sip" a bit of the Word throughout the day. It was spiritual
nourishment for him. This was another way he practiced his intimate
God connection.[58]

In the Psalms, there are numerous passages that speak of the
longing God's people have to be near him. The following one highlights
King David's longing for God. David lived one thousand years before
Christ. When Jesus was born in the flesh, he was of the bloodline of
David (see Lk. 3:23–37).

> You, God, are my God,
>   earnestly I seek you;
> I thirst for you,
>   my whole being longs for you,
> in a dry and parched land
>   where there is no water.

I have seen you in the sanctuary
and beheld your power and your glory.
Because your love is better than life,
my lips will glorify you.
I will praise you as long as I live,
and in your name I will lift up my hands.
I will be fully satisfied as with the richest of foods;
with singing lips my mouth will praise you.
On my bed I remember you;
I think of you through the watches of the night.
Because you are my help,
I sing in the shadow of your wings.
I cling to you;
your right hand upholds me. (Ps. 63:1–8)

Early in Graham's preaching career, while he was still preaching for Youth for Christ International, he accepted an invitation to speak in Wales in October of 1946. He had been to Great Britain earlier in the year with Torrey Johnson and a few others to preach in newly developed Youth for Christ chapters. There he'd met a fiery Welsh preacher by the name of Stephen Olford. Returning in October, Graham hoped to spend time with Stephen, as he'd been impressed by the spiritual fervor in his life.[59] Reverend Olford had told Billy about a renewal in his own life when he came to understand better the indwelling ministry of God the Spirit. Billy was looking to know God more deeply himself. "I was seeking for more of God in my life, and I felt that here was a man who could help me. He had a dynamic, a thrill, an exhilaration about him I wanted to capture."[60] So Billy spent two days with Olford, whose home was near Pontypridd, Wales, where Graham was preaching.

I had the privilege of hearing that story from Cliff Barrows, the longtime music and program director for the Billy Graham Evangelistic Association, over lunch one day in Atlanta. Barrows was an eyewitness to these events, as he was with Graham in Wales on that visit. Cliff related that Billy was indeed seeking to draw closer to God and that Olford was his guide. They talked and prayed during the day, pausing only in the evenings when Billy was preaching. Olford opened up passages of Scripture to Billy about the indwelling Holy Spirit and the power he provides to his people. For his part, Billy told Olford how he wanted to know and experience God through his Spirit in just these ways. Together they got on their knees in that small hotel room and prayed. Cliff said that Billy was actually prostrate on the carpet. They were both deeply affected. Soon, Billy said, "my heart is flooded with the Holy Spirit."[61] Their prayers turned from intercession to praise. Years later, Billy would write that it was Stephen Olford who most of all deepened his personal spiritual life. "I was beginning to understand that Jesus Himself was our victory, through the Holy Spirit's power," he wrote in *Just as I Am*.[62]

Billy Graham was a man who sought God in his personal life. His deep faith in God evidenced itself in the way he approached challenging situations in the ministry. Two examples from his early years will give the reader an appreciation for his trust in God to lead and guide. The first of these I might call "Bible on the Stump," from August 1949.

Few people know that Billy had a crisis of faith that lasted for a year or more. It had to do with whether a person could really trust the Bible to be true and authoritative. He preached the Bible as if it were true, but then wondered in his mind and heart if he was not being a bit naive. His friend Charles Templeton, who had also been a popular and effective evangelist with Youth for Christ, started questioning the Bible and other doctrines of evangelical faith. He shared his doubts with Billy and challenged him to read more of the latest theologians. Billy did. He read two of the heavyweights from that era, Karl Barth and Reinhold Niebuhr. Both believed in God but were more cautious about holding to the Bible as authoritative in all areas it addresses. Templeton decided he would go to Princeton Seminary to study the deeper issues. He urged Billy to go with him. Billy was interested, and in fact had always wished he'd pursued theological education at the master's and doctoral levels. But he doubted the choice of Princeton, which at that time was considered by many to be quite liberal. He offered to join Templeton if he would go to Oxford University in England instead. Together, they would spend a couple of years in theological reflection. But Templeton was set on Princeton. As months went on, their discussion and arguments over theological issues only grew. Billy found himself questioning if he was right in accepting the Bible as the Word of God.

During this time, Graham, Barrows, Grady Wilson, and Bev Shea put on an evangelistic campaign in Altoona, Pennsylvania. The team had done two campaigns in 1947, two in 1948, and were scheduled for four more in 1949, culminating in Los Angeles, which, because of its size, was frightening to Billy, especially in his current state of mind. Perhaps as a result of Billy's lack of trust and confidence, the Altoona crusade in June of 1949 did not at all go well. Grady Wilson called it "the biggest flop we've ever had anywhere."[63] Billy wondered if it was his fault.

His spirit was deeply upset by his experience in Pennsylvania as he went to Forest Home Conference Center in August of that year. There he joined many others, including Templeton, speaking at a conference for youth. The Los Angeles campaign was only a month away, and he was feeling the weight of the failure of the Altoona campaign, as well as his own spiritual battle. Forest Home, in the San Bernardino Mountains, is two hours west of downtown Los Angeles. Dr. Henrietta Mears, the gifted Bible teacher and Christian education director of Hollywood Presbyterian Church, had founded Forest Home in 1938. A strong proponent of an authoritative Bible and an evangelist in her own right, Mears was one of the most gifted educators of her generation. Under Mears's leadership, "Hollywood Pres," as it was called, grew from an average weekly attendance of about four hundred people to six thousand.

There at Forest Home, the weight on Graham's thirty-year-old soul was almost unbearable. One night, he skipped the evening meeting and went to his log cabin to be alone and read his Bible. He began to reflect. Over two thousand times the Bible states that "the Word of God came." Then he studied how often Jesus himself referred to the Bible as the Word of God. He was praying for guidance and so decided to walk in the forest and up into the mountains surrounding Forest Home. As he walked and prayed he sensed God was speaking to his spirit, calling him to trust what the Bible said about itself. He went back to his cabin, grabbed his Bible, and went back out into the moonlight. He found a tree stump, laid his Bible on it, and said, "Oh God; I cannot prove certain things. I cannot answer some of the questions Chuck is raising and some that other people are raising, but I accept this Book by faith as the word of God."[64]

He stayed by the stump praying and gently weeping as a tremendous sense of God's presence filled him. He now had a great peace that the decision he had made was right. Those months of questioning culminated as he sought God in the woods that night. He would never again question the veracity of the Bible. Perhaps as a direct result, one month later in Los Angeles, all heaven was about to break loose as he preached Jesus Christ from the Bible.[65]

The second important example of Billy's looking to God for guidance in his early ministry I might call "A Cowboy Calls and the World Listens." From September to November of 1949 Billy's faith was again rekindled. The Holy Spirit in his spirit prepared Billy for what was coming, though Billy had no idea it would be so gigantic.

The Los Angeles crusade had begun in late September. It was to be a three-week campaign. But to everyone's surprise, at almost every nightly meeting thousands of people filled the large tent in downtown Los Angeles. Hundreds were receiving Christ daily. Newspapers and radio bulletins across the country were carrying the stories. Billy called his friend Armin Gesswein, known for being a strong man of prayer and teacher on revivals, who was at Billy's offices in Minneapolis. On the phone Billy said, "Armin, you better get out here fast. Something happened and I don't know what it is. It's way beyond me."[66]

What happened next is fascinating, and demonstrates his faith in God in action. The Los Angeles committee and Billy's team wondered if the campaign should be extended. They left the decision to Billy. He'd never yet extended a campaign, but then again it had never seemed necessary. This occasion, however, seemed different. He and Barrows prayed diligently for guidance and decided to leave the decision to God. Billy asked for a sign, something that God would do to make the next steps clear to them. This is called "putting out a fleece," based on the story of Gideon in Judges 6:33–40. It's a great story. That night Billy and Cliff got their fleece! This is how it happened.

Stuart Hamblen was a massive Texan cowboy and rodeo champion who lived in greater Los Angeles. He was a legend and also a singer with a daily radio program, a contemporary of the likes of Gene Autry, John Wayne, and Roy Rogers, with whom he sometimes worked on motion pictures. Hamblen's wife was a Christian and a disciple of Mears who had been praying for Stuart for sixteen years. The son of a Methodist preacher, he had become disgusted with the faith of his childhood. He wanted little to do with God, but acquiesced to attend the Graham meetings when they first began. He rejected the message and disliked Billy Graham the more he listened to him preach. Oddly and ironically, however, Hamblen all the while encouraged his radio listeners to attend the ongoing tent meetings. On the night Cliff and Billy "put out their fleece," Hamblen was again present to hear Billy preach, but Hamblen made a scene by stomping out in the middle of the meeting. His soul was evidently in turmoil. He got himself good and drunk, went home in the middle of the night, woke his wife, and asked her to pray for him. God was bringing Stuart to the end of himself and drawing him to Jesus. He and his wife prayed together, but he was still conflicted.

Then, since Billy Graham had, by some plan known only to God, started this mess in Stuart's life, Stuart would make Billy finish it. He called and woke Billy at two in the morning, then went to Billy's lodgings and at five o'clock, after expressing many strong passions, humbly surrendered his life to Jesus Christ.[67]

Billy knew this was the fleece moment. Stuart Hamblen was converted. This was a sign that God was not finished in Los Angeles, and the campaign was extended five more weeks. Hamblen's friends noticed a change in his life. He completely quit drinking, for one thing. His friend John Wayne asked him if he had a desire to drink anymore, and when Hamblen said no Wayne told him he should write a song about his new life. The result is the wonderful gospel song "It Is No Secret (What God Can Do)," a hit single released less than two years later.[68]

After his conversion, Hamblen promoted the Los Angeles crusade even more on his radio show. He often spoke publicly about his changed life. Crowds began streaming to the event. William Randolph Hearst, the wealthy and famous newspaper magnate, was purported to have attended one of the meetings. Apparently, he informed his media empire to promote Billy Graham. Almost overnight, it seemed, Billy was a national sensation. Graham summarizes that pivotal Los Angeles experience:

> For that time, the statistics were overwhelming. In eight weeks, hundreds of thousands had heard, and thousands had responded to accept Christ as Savior; 82% of them had never been church members. Thousands more, already Christians, had come forward to register various fresh commitments to the Lord. Someone calculated that we had held seventy-two meetings. I had preached sixty-five full sermons and given hundreds of evangelistic talks to small groups, in addition to talks on the radio.[69]

The official results of the Los Angeles campaign of 1949 were 350,000 guests and 3,000 inquirers (those who made a public spiritual decision).[70] Billy goes on to say that suddenly they had gone from being a small evangelistic team to something much bigger. He was both grateful and afraid. "The whole secret of everything that happened: God answered prayer," he concluded.[71]

Those words lead me to the final point of this chapter about how Billy's personal relationship with God led him to trust God with every serious life challenge and decision. Billy would lead his organization to see that organized, fervent, habitual, prayer must undergird their work at all times. The reader might ask if prayer is some kind of a magic wand that moves God to action. No, there is no power in prayer. There is only power in God, and prayer is the primary means by which we seek him, trust him, and ask him to do what is best and right in all matters. Asking God for things in prayer is a mystery, and at the same time, something so simple that the smallest children can participate in. Does God require our prayers? No. But in his sovereignty, he chooses to use them. I like the way Dutch Sheets, a contemporary pastor and author, puts it: "A sovereign God made a sovereign choice to limit Himself in many ways and situations to the actions, decisions, and requests of human beings."[72]

In the first chapter, I told the story of how I met Billy Graham in Ottawa, Canada, in 1998. That was the first time I had the opportunity to talk personally and one-on-one with him. But earlier, in 1991, I had been a part of a group of about fifteen young evangelism leaders who met him for dinner and Q&A with Billy. The location of that meeting was his training center near Asheville, North Carolina. Each of us was prepared ahead of time to ask him one question, since his time with us was going to be limited to just one hour.

I had already begun to study his life at that time, primarily through the mentoring of his brother-in-law Leighton Ford. I knew that organized prayer preceding, during, and following an event was important to Mr. Graham. I had also read that he once said the only quantitative difference between the Los Angeles crusade of 1949 and the much smaller campaigns that preceded it was organized prayer for God to be in command and guide every element of what they said and did. "Never before did so much prayer precede and enfold a Graham Campaign," wrote John Pollack in his authorized biography of 1966.[73] Over one thousand prayer groups throughout the Los Angeles basin, as well as scores of participating local churches, began praying months before the campaign began. A twenty-four-hour around-the-clock prayer chain of men and women then covered every minute of every day. During the event, all-night prayer meetings were held in a smaller tent next to the larger tent used for the crusade itself.[74]

I'd also heard about a woman by the name of Pearl Goode, a retired school teacher and widow, who lived in Pasadena, California. She had a special sense that she was to be one of the devoted intercessors for the Los Angeles campaign. God had laid Billy and his team on her heart. Following the crusade, Pearl believed God had also called her to be one of the ongoing prayer warriors for future campaigns. Early on, she would get on a Greyhound bus traveling to a campaign site. There she would quietly check herself in to a local hotel and commence her prayers. She traveled over 48,000 miles by bus to do intercession support of this kind for the Billy Graham Evangelistic Association. Even when Graham went overseas, she was praying from a distance. When she died, Billy said he sensed the loss.[75] I read somewhere she was in attendance as a prayer warrior at forty-five campaigns/crusades.

Now, back to the dinner and Q&A in 1991. When Leighton Ford asked who wanted to ask the first question, I quickly raised my hand. I said something like, "Mr. Graham, I am told you see a strong connection between prayer and results of people finding God in your crusades. Is that correct?" His eyes lit up and for at least forty-five minutes he spoke about his relationship with God and how prayer had sustained him and been the source for much blessing on his life. He said that he had postponed crusades or canceled them if the prayer engines were not hard at work. He was passionate on this particular subject. My question, perhaps to the annoyance of some of the other young evangelists and pastors in the room, ate up most of our time together at that session!

When I was with Tom Phillips recently, he corroborated Graham's words to us that day. Tom said that the first thing Billy asked him when he was reporting on preparations for a crusade was always, "How is the prayer going?" He didn't ask about money raised or churches and leaders involved until after the prayer question.[76]

Billy Graham had an intimate connection with God to the end of his life. He loved God, trusted God, and called on God with millions of others to bring people throughout the world to a personal relationship with Jesus Christ. His relationship with God was always the core reason for his being. It prepared him, sustained him, and comforted him in times of trouble. That's why he so longed for people to personally know the God who has loved us and invited us to know him.

If you have not done so, I hope you will take the steps necessary to personally know God too. We all need to come to Jesus Christ. In prayer, tell him you desire to know him and that you want him to lead your life. Ask him to forgive all your sins and to make you one of his own children. He will do it. He loves you.

SIX

ALL HEAVEN
BREAKS LOOSE

Jesus went through all the towns and villages
. . . proclaiming the good news of the kingdom
and healing every disease and sickness. When
he saw the crowds, he had compassion on them,
because they were harassed and helpless, like
sheep without a shepherd.
—*Matthew 9:35–36*

———

Go into all the world and preach the gospel
to all creation.
—*Mark 16:15*

———

I've never seen such a hunger in people for
spiritual things. . . . People realize the past is
gone, the future is uncertain, and the present
seems to be hopeless.

—BILLY GRAHAM[77]

L os Angeles was the place where all heaven broke loose. Billy Graham and his team had been used to smaller venues with fewer results. After Los Angeles in 1949, that all changed. The event launched the national and international ministry of Billy Graham. This ministry would then span six more decades from the 1950s through 2005. This chapter is a whirlwind look at those nearly sixty years of life and work. This book is not meant to be a comprehensive account of Billy's life and ministry—it would take a team of people and many thousands of pages in order to do that! More appropriately, I think, this chapter will display God at work in Graham's life in three major ways. The first is through the campaigns, which later came to be called crusades. The second is through his books, magazines, newspapers, radio, and television. And the third is the many ways that the Billy Graham Association met, influenced, and sometimes partnered with leaders in government, industry, media, and entertainment.

The totals gathered from the Los Angeles meetings of September 15 to November 20, 1949, suggested a new paradigm was emerging. Approximately 350,000 people had attended. More than 3,000 had made spiritual decisions to come to Christ or return to him. Billy had preached sixty-five times in the tent, which held 6,000 and was then expanded to hold 9,000. In addition, he spoke at scores and scores of smaller meetings during the daytime all over greater Los Angeles. Even well-known people in business and entertainment came to faith, or at least were drawn a step closer. You've already read of the singing cowboy Stuart Hamblen. Jim Vaus, who was connected to the gangster Mickey Cohen, also came to faith. So did Louis Zamperini, the Olympic athlete who during World War II had suffered terrible torture in a Japanese prisoner camp. His story was told in the 2010 book and 2014 film adaptation *Unbroken*. Vaus and Zamperini and thousands like them were transformed into new people by receiving Jesus Christ into their lives.

Why was Los Angeles 1949 so successful? As I explored in the last chapter, Graham felt that prayer was the major reason for what happened in Los Angeles. But there are at least two other reasons worth mentioning.

First, the country was only four years beyond World War II when the crusade took place, and people were again facing new, frightening global realities. Just one month before Los Angeles, in answer to American actions in Japan at the close of the war, the Russians detonated an atomic bomb. Those of us raised during the Cold War remember the fear of total annihilation. We trained for it by hiding under our desks during drills at school! And, only six days after the Los Angeles campaign began, Communists in China overthrew the ruling government. The Red Menace of a Communist China was upon us. People were deeply unsettled. The American dream of a safe, wholesome, prosperous life, which they thought was secured after the Second World War, was again in jeopardy. At times of geopolitical unrest, people are more willing to look for spiritual guidance and answers.

The second reason, in my opinion, was that God chose to use Billy Graham, with many others, to bring what Christians call revival to the land. Throughout the millennia, there have been God-ordained seasons of greater openness to God, when a greater number of people have come to meet Christ, finding the secret to eternal life. We call these momentous moments times of revival. In many ways, Los Angeles

1949, led by the growing but still young ministry of Billy Graham, was what initiated a global revival.

Of course, that is what I write now, with the benefit of hindsight. Billy didn't know at the time, while he was living in the midst of that moment, that this was about to happen. He wondered if the experience in Los Angeles was a one-time phenomenon. But within three months he would see it was not. Boston would be next, then London, then New York, Australia, and New Zealand, and over the next six decades, nearly 400 campaigns in 99 countries of the world to more than 215 million people.[78] In addition, he made shorter visits to other nations so that today the Billy Graham Evangelistic Association reports that Billy has preached the Good News of Jesus Christ in more than 185 nations.[79] Taken together, those six decades of evangelistic preaching yielded more than three million decisions for Christ.[80]

Billy would be back in Los Angeles in the years to come. I recently watched the annual football game between the University of Southern California (USC) and the University of California at Los Angeles (UCLA), held in the famed Los Angeles Coliseum. At one point in the game, as the cameras panned the stadium, one focused on a bronze plaque hanging on one of its walls. It listed the most illustrious events of that illustrious stadium. There on the plaque I could read "Billy Graham Crusade 1963—134,254 persons," referring to the tremendous Los Angeles Crusade that Graham would hold there fourteen years after the first Los Angeles campaign. That event was the largest recorded attendance in the history of the coliseum, which has held Super Bowls, the Rose Bowl, Summer Olympics, and more. During every campaign and crusade, the star was always Jesus Christ, as all heaven broke loose.

I can't think of a better illustration of the meteoric rise of Billy Graham and his message and ministry of Jesus Christ than the writing on that plaque in the Los Angeles Coliseum. Los Angeles 1949 filled a tent that was expanded to hold nine thousand. Los Angeles 1963 filled the coliseum that held 134,000.

In 1946, the Gallup organization began a yearly survey of the ten most admired men and women anywhere in the world. In 1946–1949, Billy Graham was largely unknown, so we shouldn't expect to see his name on such a list. But from 1950 to 2016 he is in the top ten sixty times. Sixty times in sixty-six years. How does he compare to others? Queen Elizabeth is mentioned forty-eight times; President Ronald Reagan, thirty-one times; Pope John Paul II, twenty-seven times; and President Jimmy Carter, twenty-six mentions. That is a rather illustrious group and, most would argue, very worthy of admiration. But none approach the enduring admiration given to Billy Graham. And remember, Graham has been out of the public eye for the last decade. Still, he is usually in the top ten.

Why did this happen? Historians debate the reasons. I find the ideas of Grant Wacker in his book *America's Pastor* to be intriguing in this regard. He postulates that in the American mind, Billy Graham was a model, almost an archetype of the American ideal. He was a noble man of high values, a family man, loyal to his wife always. He was tall, handsome, and athletic. He had answers for the angst Americans faced in the post–World War II era as new menaces arose. He represented common decency and the American dream of a person who rose far above his station in life. He was aw-shucks humble and never claimed to be anything himself. He always pointed to his Lord Jesus Christ. Listeners were drawn to these notions and saw in Graham that they were more than ideas. They could be lived out. Wacker says that "Graham's audiences represent the kind of ordered world one might imagine on a Norman Rockwell cover."[81] He ends his book with a similar thought: "The preacher from North Carolina touched their memories and called them to be the kind of people they knew they ought to be. Often they failed, and sometimes he did too, but perfection was never the point."[82]

Join me now on a whirlwind tour of the last six decades of Billy Graham's work spreading the evangelistic message of Jesus Christ. You are in for a ride.

Our first stop, Boston. A large church in Boston invited Billy to speak over New Year's, 1950. The invitation had been made and accepted long before the Los Angeles campaign and its breakthrough. Neither Graham nor the church led by the well-known Pastor Harold John Ockenga thought the pandemonium that erupted in Los Angeles would happen in Boston as well.

Boston was the recognized center of education in the United States, home to legendary schools such as Harvard, MIT, Tufts, and Boston Latin. US presidents, Supreme Court justices, and Nobel Prize winners were graduates of schools such as these. It was also a place steeped in history—the New England heritage of Puritans, but also sophisticated Boston Brahmins. Surely evangelical Christian displays of revival and emotionalism would never happen in Boston. Both men were wrong. The church was overwhelmed with people, so much so that Pastor Ockenga had to quickly secure Mechanics Hall in the center of

Boston's historic district in order to accommodate the crowds. Surely its several-thousand-person capacity would be more than adequate. But it wasn't. Finally, they secured the even larger Boston Garden, home of the Boston Celtics of Bob Cousy and Red Auerbach. What was intended to be a set of meetings in a local church was suddenly Boston and New England–wide.

One reason for the expansion was the media. The media swarm in Los Angeles was duplicated in New England. They had begun to attach themselves to what was happening. There was a story to tell. For his part, Billy was concerned that the sophisticated reporters and journalists would be less friendly in Boston than they had been in California. New England was not then, and I suppose is still not often considered an area where Christian spirituality is robust. But God took care of that too.

I remember hearing a wonderful story about this from Allan Emery, a successful businessman and one of Graham's strongest, early supporters. We were together at a board meeting in 1999 when Emery told me how just before Billy was scheduled to address the New England press and respond to their questions, a telegram arrived from Los Angeles. Emery took the telegram as Graham was preparing for the press. The telegram, he said, was from a Hollywood producer offering Billy the starring role in two movies with a guaranteed contract of two million dollars. Allan felt he should give the telegram to Billy before the press conference just in case he wanted to send a response. Billy read it. His response was to immediately wad it into a ball to throw away, but since he had to get to the reporters he put the wad in his suit pocket and stepped into the media lights to face the cameras and questioners.

I wish I remembered more of the story, but I do recall that at some point in the press conference one of the reporters asked a rather denigrating question. He asked how Billy would respond to the assertion that he was in the mass evangelism business for fame and fortune. By way of context, it is important to remember that the country was still then living with a prevalent "Elmer Gantry" view of evangelists and their work and motives. *Elmer Gantry* was a popular, satirical 1926 novel by Sinclair Lewis portraying a fundamentalist evangelist who was motivated in his work by the very things he preached against in public: money, alcohol, and fornication. Lewis even won the Nobel Prize in Literature three years after the novel was published.

The reporter's pungent question certainly presumed a great deal. Emery said that Billy paused. Then he reached into his pocket and pulled out the crumpled, wadded up telegram and said something to the effect of, "I guess if I was in this work for the reasons you suggest I wouldn't have wadded up this telegram to throw in the trash as soon as this gathering is done." He handed the reporter the telegram still in its crumpled condition. The man opened it up, read it, and then without a word passed it to the reporter sitting next to him. It made the rounds that day, and no one questioned Billy's motives after that. Boston was a success rivaling Los Angeles. The Boston press would remain, from that day forward, generally favorable to Billy Graham his whole life.

Los Angeles and now Boston: this was no fluke. Would it, however, be international? Churches in Great Britain inquired as to whether Billy would come and preach across the pond. He agreed. Other US crusades continued, with strong support and results, but preparations began for London and Great Britain, which would take place in 1954. Once again, the organization of massive prayer preceding the crusade was deemed most essential. More than three thousand prayer groups began interceding almost immediately after the crusade was announced and scheduled.

There were, of course, challenges. The first was Billy's speaking style. His rapid pace and dramatic delivery wouldn't be well received by the more reserved Brits. He sought to slow down and lose some of his dramatics. The more damaging challenge was from a mistake made in a promotional prayer calendar printed in the United States. It stated that England was a place where socialism was then rampant. The brochure said, "What Hitler's bombs could not do, socialism with its accompanying evils shortly accomplished."[83] Media and government in Britain were incensed. It took weeks for that furor to calm down.

The crusade in England commenced March 1, 1954, and went on for nearly twelve weeks. At first the meeting site was north London and Harringay Stadium, which could hold 11,400 people. But attendance quickly averaged more than 12,000 nightly. The final meeting in England was held May 22 on a cold and wet night in Wembley Stadium, which was capable of holding up to 120,000 people. It was packed that night. Throngs of people remained outside unable to enter because of the crowds. By the time the crusade ended, more than 2 million had attended. More than 38,000 people came forward, and over 50 percent of the British people who made those spiritual decisions replied that they had no regular church involvement.[84] The ministry of Billy and his team was now an international phenomenon. God was on the move.

Next, let's visit Berlin. Germany and Berlin in 1954 were of special importance because of their geopolitical centrality in European affairs before, during, and after World War II. The Cold War was quietly seething, and East and West Berlin often seemed to be at the center of those troubles. The Berlin Wall was not yet built—it wouldn't be until 1961—and so when Billy preached in the western half of the city, thousands of East Berliners were able to cross the border to hear him. More than 80,000 attended the one-day event in Berlin in 1954. Over 16,000 response cards indicating a spiritual decision were mailed to the follow-up center because the stadium, which had once served the Nazis and Hitler as the Olympic stadium, didn't allow people to walk forward onto the infield.[85] The follow-up team discerned that many of the cards that came by post were not actual spiritual decisions but simply people signing up for whatever was asked. Yet, even if some of the cards were not spiritual decisions, the fact that people took the time to send a card suggests that many others who did not may have also made decisions. Any way one looks at it, it was a massive response. The 16,000 represent a 20 percent decisional rate, which far exceeded the general average of approximately 5 percent.[86] German people, perhaps more than many others, knew that they needed God to make life right. Governments and economies and wars cannot do it.

The crusade in New York City in 1957 could be a book all on its own. When Billy first accepted the invitation from Protestant church leaders to come to the Big Apple, he knew he was in many respects entering uncharted waters. Like London, New York was huge and largely irreligious. Nearly 60 percent of New Yorkers claimed no religious affiliation at that time.[87] Even more challenging was the ethnic diversity of New York. More than sixty minority groups inhabited its five boroughs. A later chapter of this book will be dedicated to ethnic and racial diversity and Billy Graham, but suffice it to say his friendship and partnership with the Reverend Martin Luther King Jr. was made public to the world in New York City.

Madison Square Garden, holding nearly 20,000 souls, was secured for the New York crusade starting May 15. The plan was to be there for six weeks. But as in Los Angeles, Boston, and London, it would become necessary to extend their stay—through September 1. Overflow crowds filled the Garden almost every night from the beginning. Rallies held independently from the Garden meetings in Brooklyn, Wall Street, Times Square, the Bronx, the United Nations, and various universities added to the swelling numbers. Again, media played a huge role. During the crusade an opportunity to televise the Saturday-night events on the ABC network brought 6.5 million households throughout the United States to the crusade.[88] Graham realized that one ABC broadcast viewership was equivalent to a year's worth of full Madison Square Garden crowds. If there was any doubt of the national prominence of Billy Graham, it was ended that year in New York. He was then a national celebrity, even though he personally hated the attention.

By the time the New York crusade of 1957 concluded, more than 2 million people had attended the meetings and 61,000 had registered spiritual decisions. If we also count the decisions received from the television broadcasts, the total was 86,000 commitments to Jesus Christ. Those numbers are daunting, so let me share one story Graham tells in *Just as I Am*:

> One night a plainly dressed woman stood in the inquiry room with tears running down her cheeks as she asked Christ to come into her life. When her counselor asked if there was anything else she wanted to share, she replied that she was very afraid of her son. "He drinks a lot," she said, "and I'm

afraid he may beat me when he finds out I've become a Christian." Before the counselor could speak, a voice nearby called out, "It's okay, Mom. I'm here too."[89]

There were 86,000 stories like that in 1957. Such stories continue all over the world every day. I once heard that over 75,000 people meet Christ every day. I don't know how that number was determined, but I believe it's in the ballpark. The passionate, loving God is drawing people who were once far away from him, toward him. If you feel a need to connect with God, stop reading and ask him now. Simply pray something like this:

God, I need you.
Forgive me for all my sins.
I commit my life to you and ask you to make me one of your
      children, forever.
Amen.

A prayer like that, prayed in sincerity, is more than enough to begin or return to a personal relationship with our Lord. The Bible promises he will never leave or forsake you (see Heb. 13:5).

The New York City crusade was exhausting for Billy. He ran out of existing sermons, and for the last weeks of the meetings was writing new ones daily. He also carried the weight of the finances required, the stress on his whole staff as the meetings continued, and an increasing compassion for all who came looking for God and God's help. In a very personal moment in his autobiography he shares the prayer he offered God during this stress-filled time: "Oh God you have to do it, I can't do it. I just can't do it."[90] He goes on to say that God met his every need. I'll tell you why I share this story. I'm always tempted to elevate men and women I respect to hero status. Yet we're all just human. Billy Graham shows us that while on the outside he appeared to be a hero, he wasn't. I often say that a grown-up is merely a child in an adult body. We are all dependent on something or someone, and those things and those persons will inevitably let us down. Billy was dependent on God. I am too, most of the time. There is nothing shameful about that. It's simply true. I often hear skeptics say that Christians use God for a crutch. There's nothing wrong with that when you know you are crippled without him.

Now, I have placed the spotlight on four among nearly four hundred crusades and campaigns Graham held over six decades. There were others of great significance, such as 1959 in Australia and New Zealand, where he spoke in five major cities. It is estimated that by the time the event ended, over half the population of those countries heard the Good News of Jesus Christ.[91] Then, in 1973 in Korea, his largest series of meetings ever took place. Over five days, he preached to three million attendees. On the final day, he preached to more than one million people sitting on the airport tarmac in three-foot-square outlined spaces. This just may have been the largest gathering of people ever to hear a religious message.[92]

Did he stay humble through all of this? It appears so. He had a spiritual compass reminding him that he was only God's messenger for a particular period of time. A friend tells the story of Billy, Cliff Barrows, and George Beverly Shea coming to my friend's parents' house one night after a crusade. It was San Francisco 1958, and Mike Holmgren, the NFL coach and executive, is the friend. Mike was not yet ten at this time. His father was the pastor of a little church in San Francisco during the time of the crusade. Billy's evangelistic team accepted an invitation to come to Mike's parents' home where they had coffee and sweets. Mike's fondest memory was watching the team along with his parents and his siblings singing hymns together at the piano late into the night. That suggests that Billy enjoyed us regular folk just as well as queens and presidents.

⁂

His crusades in the 1970s, '80s, and '90s would only grow in size and continue to build in spiritual impact. I will close this section on his large public meetings with a brief story from the very last one.

By this time, I was working at the Graham Center at Wheaton College. I attended thirteen crusades from 1998 to 2005. On this final occasion, my daughter Courtney went with me. She was seventeen at the time, and I promised to show her New York City. We were in Times Square and Broadway on Sunday morning. It was crowded with people from all over the world even at that time of the day. Our plan was to visit the popular Manhattan tourist sites, then take the subway to Queens, where Billy's final public meeting would be held in the afternoon. It was a miserably hot day. At one point, I looked at the crowds and thought to myself, I wish these people were all heading out to hear Billy Graham. When we boarded the subway in Times Square it was already pretty full. I can't remember if we were able to get a seat. I figured, however, that the farther we traveled from Times Square more and more people would get off and we would likely be more comfortable with the extra space. We did soon get seats, but not many people seemed to be getting off. I was surprised. I was then even more surprised as I noticed that more and more people were boarding the train. I wondered where they were all going. Before long, it looked like the United Nations in our subway car. Soon there were not only no seats, but no room even to stand.

When we finally arrived at the crusade site, in Flushing Meadow, where the 1964 World's Fair had been held, thousands of people were emptying out of the subway cars. Most carried folding chairs and food and water with them. A multicolored, massive amount of people was coming to hear Billy Graham. This ranked as one of the most multiethnic events in the city's history.[93]

There were nearly 100,000 people there that day. The three-day event would exceed 200,000 souls. The tired warrior was now eighty-seven years old, and to us it felt like the whole world wanted to hear him talk about his hero, Jesus Christ. In Queens in 2005, Billy was no longer a fiery orator. He was a grandfather speaking to the generations. His invitation to come to Jesus Christ was met by streaming numbers going forward in the blistering New York City summer heat. Billy was growing old, but his message was as fresh and vibrant as a summer sunrise.

Not only was the influence of Billy Graham felt by those who heard him preach live or in person, but also he was gifted with the written word, and with a unique ability to explain faith to an often-distrusting media.

On one occasion, I was with Graham and his chief of staff, David Bruce, in Billy's home in Montreat, North Carolina. I presented Billy with a small book I had written. He wanted me to have one of his as well, so he gave me a signed copy of *Peace with God*. It was his first book, and I believe it is still his best seller at two million copies. He wrote it with Ruth's help in 1953.[94] *Peace with God* has been called "a theology for the common man."[95] Billy told me that when he and Ruth finished the manuscript, he sent it to his pastor-scholar friend Donald Grey Barnhouse. Barnhouse was the pastor, then, of the prestigious and historical Tenth Avenue Presbyterian Church in Philadelphia. Billy asked Pastor Barnhouse to review the manuscript and make suggestions for improvement. Then, with a twinkle in his eye and a big smile, he remembered: "Barnhouse returned it with more notes and suggestions than I had words in the original text!" So, he said, "We just published it the way we wrote it."

When I first read *Peace with God*, I was impressed by the level of his theological sophistication at such a young age of thirty-five. It is a tremendous book. The themes he addresses resonate in all his thirty other books from that time onward. You hear the same themes in his sermons. I know, and have written earlier, that Graham regretted not doing more formal postgraduate study. But *Peace with God* indicates the sharpness of his mind and the comprehensive nature of his theology. I believe his expansive reading and engagement with theologians over the years only increased his brilliance. Sometimes people emphasize the simplicity of his writing and preaching, but I believe it was simplicity on the other side of complexity that he possessed. This made him able to relate truths to untrained listeners in ways they could understand.

Beyond his public preaching and book publishing, Billy Graham and the Billy Graham Evangelistic Association (BGEA) moved decisively into multiple media pursuits beginning in the 1950s. Radio came first. Billy believed that a radio broadcast would have the opportunity to reach many more people in their homes than he could ever preach in person. God brought Billy people familiar with radio, and together they began to pursue a program. But the start-up money was a problem. The American Broadcasting Company (ABC) offered a thirteen-week, Sunday-afternoon, thirty-minute time slot at a cost of $92,000. That was an astronomical amount of money. The Christian promoters of the idea felt that if Billy could start by raising $25,000, that would cover start-up costs and pay at least for the first three weeks of airtime. The team was in Portland holding a crusade during this time. Billy called everyone together for a prayer meeting. The team and the radio promoters got on their knees. One of the radio promoters, Fred Dienert, remembers the gist of the prayer Billy prayed:

> Lord, you know I'm doing all that I can. You know I don't have any money, but I believe we ought to do this. You know Lord, I have a mortgage on that little house in Montreat. Lord, I'll put another mortgage on; I'll take the little I have and put another mortgage on. Lord, I don't know where the money is, and if I did know where it is, I'm too busy to go out and get it. I feel the burden for it, but it's up to You, and if You want this I want You to give me a sign. And I'm going to put out the fleece. And the fleece is for the $25,000 to come in by midnight [tonight].[96]

Billy did not announce the need at the crusade that night in Portland, not until after the offering was taken at the very end, for crusade expenses. Once it was collected, he spoke to the audience about the radio possibility. He told people that if they were interested in helping, he and his team would be in the back office after the service that night. Shoeboxes would be ready to receive any financial assistance people might want to offer. People responded beyond all human expectations. Twenty-three thousand five hundred dollars were given that night, placed in those simple shoeboxes. Many of the team and the radio people were thrilled, but Billy reminded them that the fleece was for $25,000. The radio promoters offered to make up the difference, but Graham refused. It looked like no radio ministry. God must have another plan.

However, when Billy and the evangelistic team returned to the hotel that night there were three envelopes waiting for them. The envelopes were placed there by a person who had waited in the long line at the stadium but then had given up waiting. Fifteen hundred dollars were in those envelopes. The Billy Graham Radio Fund was started.[97] A weekly radio program was soon started, called the *Hour of Decision*, which at its zenith reached into twenty million American homes every Sunday afternoon. It is one of the most popular religious radio programs in history.[98]

Billy and his organization also went on to produce two magazines and one daily newspaper. All three publications are still in circulation. *Christianity Today* was founded in 1956, targeted at Christian thinkers and pastors, offering strong, theological foundations for the growing number of Christian evangelicals in America. It remains today the most influential magazine of its kind. *Christianity Today* was quickly handed off and turned into its own company, though Graham and his representatives chaired the board as well. I believe that there may still be a BGEA representative on the board today. In 1960, another magazine was started, called *Decision*. *Decision* was designed to be more of a *Reader's Digest* piece, offering devotions, Bible teaching, and stories of interest to Christians of all shapes and sizes. At its height, it had a circulation of over six million.[99] I have had the wonderful privilege of writing a few articles for *Decision*.

Then there was the popular Billy Graham newspaper column, "My Answer," which circulated in newspapers throughout America. In the 1960s and 1970s this column of spiritual and theological advice reached more than twenty million Americans every week. Today, it is still in over two hundred newspapers.[100] Graham oversaw the column for many years, but also had trusted team members do most of the writing. I still find it helpful for dealing with the issues of the day.

The Billy Graham Evangelistic Association ventured into film-making, and later other forms of visual transmission of sermons. World Wide Pictures was started in 1951 as a production and distribution company for Christian films, a subsidiary of the BGEA. This opportunity can also be traced back to Portland, Oregon, in 1950, when a documentary was made about Billy and that crusade. The power of movies to reach people was growing, and Billy and others sensed keenly how God could use this new medium. They produced more than one hundred feature-length films, starting with *Mr. Texas*, the first Christian Western, in 1951, with a cast that included Billy Graham playing himself!

I remember going to several of these films in the 1970s and 1980s. Often local churches would rent a movie theater and promote the films throughout the area. In each of the films, Graham came on-screen and summarized the gospel message at the end. Usually Christians from local churches were trained to follow up with people making spiritual decisions at the films. That was of course their purpose: to save souls.

A good friend of mine, Paul Knight, gave his life to Christ at a World Wide Pictures film. He is today one of the leading pastors in the state of North Dakota. His church preaches and shares the gospel with great effect, reaching hundreds of people every year.

Forty-four years after making the first evangelistic film, the BGEA would attempt to reach the whole world through satellite technology. In March of 1995, Billy would preach a crusade in Puerto Rico. The transmission would be broadcast to 185 countries and territories, translated into 116 languages. The name given to this daunting technological project was "Global Mission." Billy wrote, "It may have been the most extensive single evangelistic outreach in the history of the Church."[101] One estimate is that the transmissions were heard by over one billion people.[102] Only God knows how many of those people met Jesus Christ. His message is for the whole world. I find great comfort in believing that no human on earth escapes the awareness and love of God.

Further developments in communication technologies would lead to the "My Hope" campaigns in the first two decades of our new century. My Hope was developed to bring Billy Graham into homes through DVD. Christians all over the world invited their pre-Christian friends, family, neighbors, and coworkers to sit in their homes and hear a special message from Billy. The messages were combined with testimonies of well-known people who had embraced Jesus. Then the Christian hosts would share their testimonies with their guests. My wife and I hosted a My Hope meeting. Many of our neighbors accepted our invitation, and now, years later, we have closer friendships with them and more opportunities for spiritual discussion. I don't know how many millions of people heard the gospel in My Hope living rooms around the world, but God does, and that is what matters.

Finally, the latest mass-media outreach has been through Internet and digital technology. Graham's organization has linked with several others around the world to offer the gospel twenty-four hours a day via the SearchforJesus.net website. If you enter the BGEA headquarters in Charlotte, North Carolina, today, a large screen greets you and displays what is happening through this format. When I was recently there, the screen read that 122 people from around the world were at that moment online watching and listening to the gospel. It also read that through this global outreach, 10,899,808 people had already indicated decisions for Christ.

Each of these media ventures further established and kept Billy Graham's name and, more importantly, allowed Billy's message of salvation through Jesus Christ to influence people in a variety of ways.

One thing that most everyone knows about Billy Graham, if they know anything at all about him, is that he was friends with certain world leaders and celebrities. This is what I call the third dimension of his public presence.

Starting with the Los Angeles campaign of 1949, the mass media was fascinated with Billy. Print, radio, and television networks followed him almost everywhere. Part of the reason for this was his association with famous people. Billy knew and met, for instance, with eleven sitting presidents, starting with Harry Truman. He played golf with most of them, and was a pastor to many of them. When Billy traveled internationally, soon other heads of state wanted to meet with him as well. In the 1950s, he met with Winston Churchill, and also began a lifelong friendship with Queen Elizabeth II. The queen and Graham met together on twelve occasions.[103] One of those meetings has recently been highlighted on the popular Netflix television show *The Crown*. Graham's relationships with US presidents have also been well documented in an excellent book by Nancy Gibbs and Michael Duffy, *The Preacher and the Presidents*. Four of them became what might be called close friends: Lyndon B. Johnson, Richard M. Nixon, George H. W. Bush, and George W. Bush. I will write more about the relationship between Billy and President Nixon in a later chapter, because it became one of the great sorrows of Billy's life.

Celebrities were drawn to him too. In 1963, when he preached his second Los Angeles campaign, a whole section of seats was set aside for Hollywood stars and moguls. The actress Debbie Reynolds invited twenty top-rank film stars to meet Billy privately for a question-and-answer session on spiritual matters. The gathering lasted four hours. At the closing gathering of that campaign, held in the mammoth Los Angeles Coliseum, where more than 134,000 people attended and another 20,000 were left outside for safety reasons, comedian and actor Jack Benny, who attended one of the meetings and sensed the difference of the occasion, remarked, "I can't get over it. These people are so quiet. I've never seen anything like it."[104]

Leighton Ford shared the story with me about Muhammed Ali and Billy. Leighton met Ali in an airport and asked if he would be interested in meeting Billy Graham. The boxer responded with an enthusiastic "Yes!" As most readers know, the Champ was not only a great athlete, he was a deeply devoted Muslim. The meeting was arranged between them, with the press following close behind, in North Carolina at Billy's home. But since the Graham home is in the mountains above the little town of Montreat, and is only accessible by a gate, the press could not come up the hill. According to Leighton, the two had a wonderful discussion, and when Ali came back down the hill he was asked by the press what Billy's home was like. He responded, "It's just the kind of home you'd expect a man of God to have." Graham's home is not a mansion, but simply a large mountain cabin that looks very lived in. I've been with Billy in his family room, his kitchen, and his study. It is a warm, family home. Ali saw that and was impressed.

Titans of business also met with Billy and supported him in every aspect of his work. For example, John D. MacArthur, the insurance tycoon, offered Billy one thousand acres in Palm Beach Gardens, Florida, as well as one million dollars of his own money, to build a university with Billy's name. The idea was to build a place where young people could obtain an Ivy League–quality education with evangelical theology undergirding it. After long wrestling in prayer, Graham realized that this would divert his energies from his primary calling of evangelism, and he declined.[105]

There were others as well. Dr. Sterling Huston, one of Billy's close associates and also a precious mentor to me in my years at the Graham Center, told me of a dinner Graham had with the oil tycoon J. Harold Pew, of Sun Oil Company, in his home. Pew had been a major donor to the launch of *Christianity Today* magazine in 1956.[106] He had also put up the front money to broadcast the New York crusade of 1957 on ABC television.[107] A bit of background might be necessary to understand this dinner: Billy and his pastor-scholar friend from Boston, Harold

John Ockenga, were both on the board of Fuller Theological Seminary in Pasadena, California, at the time. They found themselves wishing that a great seminary like Fuller could be birthed on the East Coast. That dream would become Gordon-Conwell Theological Seminary, founded in 1969. Evidently, Pew was a strong believer in education, and Billy had spoken with him in detail about the new school. At the dinner, with both Mr. and Mrs. Pew, Billy was ready to get up from the table following the meal when Harold Pew said, "Billy, before you get up, look under your plate." He did so and found a very large check to help launch the new seminary. Billy was filled with gratitude, but Pew was not yet done. He said, "Billy, now look under my wife's plate." Billy did, and another check for the same amount was found there. Such was the generosity of J. Harold Pew and others like him for the cause of Christ in the world.

What is it exactly that drew the powerful, rich, and famous to Billy Graham? Many people have wondered, and many have speculated. I am told that it was three qualities they discovered in the evangelist. First, his spiritual commitment to God was foremost in his life. The powerful, rich, and the famous are often looking for meaning and purpose beyond their achievements, and often they long for God's help. On the night that President George H. W. Bush authorized the attack on Iraq in 1991, which it was fairly certain would be regarded a stunning victory for American forces and the commander in chief, he asked Billy to spend the night in the White House and be in prayer with him and Mrs. Bush. Billy did.

Second, people of status were probably drawn to Graham because he had the capacity to "fill the room." Some people simply have that quality, and Billy was one of them. His stature, looks, and manner made people want to be with him. He could command a room without even knowing it.

Finally, Billy's profound humility, which I wrote about in chapter 1, was a comfort to famous and powerful people. He was not out to replace them or compete with them. He simply enjoyed being with them, and though he was made a celebrity by the success of his work and his associations, he came across as someone not needing or wanting to be. I remember a story told me by one of Billy's closest staff associates, Dr. John Akers. Akers told me about a time when he accompanied Graham to a meeting of the leading Christians in the world. As others were jockeying for where to sit around the table, Graham walked in quietly, found his name tag, put it on (as if it was needed!), turned to the leader next to him, and said, "Hello, my name is Billy Graham." Now that's humility.

I do know this much: Billy was as surprised by his notoriety as anyone. Perhaps it was because of his simple farm upbringing. In the early days of his rise to fame, he would upon returning to the farm in Charlotte gather the family around him. His younger sister Jean says he would talk for hours about the places he'd been and the people whom he'd met. He was as surprised as anybody by it all. All of that attention would also, before long, feel costly to him. One time while passing a little church in Black Mountain, North Carolina, not far from Billy's home, Billy turned to David Bruce and said, "Being a pastor of a little church is all I really wanted to be." I think he was sad when he said that.

SEVEN
RACIAL JUSTICE, PEACE NOT WAR, HUMAN SUFFERING

After this I looked, and there before me was a great multitude that no one could count, from every nation, tribe, people and language, standing before the throne and before the Lamb. They were wearing white robes and were holding palm branches in their hands. And they cried out in a loud voice:

> "Salvation belongs to our God
> who sits on the throne,
> and to the Lamb."
> —*Revelation 7:9–10*

———

Jesus was not a white man; he was not a black man. He came from that part of the world that touches Africa and Asia and Europe. Christianity is not a white man's religion and don't let anybody ever tell you that it's white or black. Christ belongs to all people; he belongs to the whole world.

— BILLY GRAHAM[108]

———

Much of my life has been a pilgrimage—constantly learning, changing, growing and maturing. I have come to see in deeper ways some of the implications of my faith and message, not the least of which is in the area of human rights and racial and ethnic understanding.

—BILLY GRAHAM[109]

This chapter is written especially for people in their twenties and thirties, though we older folks will appreciate it as well. Did Billy Graham only preach the gospel of the new birth? Or did he and his organization also seek justice and the alleviation of need in our world? There is no question that Billy's main calling was to restore the vertical relationship between people and God. During the fight for civil rights, he once said, "The race question will not be solved by demonstrations in the streets, but in the hearts of both Negro and white. There must be genuine love to replace prejudice and hate. This love can be supplied by Christ and only by Christ."[110] He always believed that the new birth was essential to create a new kind of human, who could live by love only by being filled with God's love. Only then would hate and prejudice be overcome.

But preaching and living according to the gospel of Jesus Christ also includes pursuing justice and alleviating human suffering in the horizontal dimensions of life. I thank God that people in their twenties and thirties often care so much about this, because those of us who are older too easily forget about it. The theological idea behind this is bringing the good kingdom of God to every dimension of human life. The first words uttered by Jesus Christ in the Gospel of Mark are these: "The time is fulfilled, and the kingdom of God is at hand; repent and believe in the gospel" (Mk. 1:15 ESV). Jesus is expanding on what the coming of God's kingdom means in the Gospel of Luke:

The Spirit of the Lord is upon me,

    because he has anointed me

    to proclaim good news to the poor.

He has sent me to proclaim liberty to the captives

    and recovering of sight to the blind,

    to set at liberty those who are oppressed,

    to proclaim the year of the Lord's favor. (Lk. 4:18–19 ESV)

The kingdom Jesus speaks of is a new world order under his leadership, where right triumphs over evil. It was displayed vividly in his time on earth. The hungry were filled; the blind, lame, and diseased were healed. The elements such as raging storms were stilled. Even death was reversed in his presence. Those few years while he was incarnated into a fully human and fully divine being were a magnified picture of what God wants to do and is doing now on his earth through his church, through his people, and through his common grace poured out on the world. The kingdom of God is at hand. Hard to believe?

The media is not very good at sharing good news, since they know how our heads turn more quickly to see or hear what's bad, or what makes us scared. Therefore, it is easy to think much more is wrong than right in our world. But just this morning I watched the report of an apartment fire in New York City. Many died, but the little-known story is of the man who went back into the building and rescued four families. God is on the move in his world.

Perhaps a personal word is acceptable here. While I was writing this book, and Christmas 2017 was approaching, I learned that I have a rather rare and aggressive liver cancer. Many are praying for my immediate healing, and I would like that too. I have seen it happen in others.

But far more often the God of the kingdom uses advancing science in the field of cancer treatments to bring about a good end. He can save people suffering from cancer by the prayers of friends as well as by the developments of medicine supported by prayer. I'm deeply grateful for both, and I know that advances in medical sciences are bringing wholeness and life to many. These are God's graces too. In all spheres of society and human existence, God is at work through his creation.

Early on, Billy Graham came to realize that racism was and is a deep injustice in our culture and that he had to do something about it. He was a contemporary of the Reverend Martin Luther King Jr., and their friendship helped each of them grow.

One day, I was walking from my hotel in Jackson, Mississippi, to Belhaven College, where I was serving as a member of the board of directors. I passed an open-air stadium that could hold several thousand people, though it had not been maintained over the years. I asked Belhaven's president what the stadium's purpose was. He said, "That is where Billy Graham preached in 1952. It is also where he first pulled down the ropes of separation between blacks and whites."[111] Now, there is some conjecture among scholars as to whether he "pulled down the ropes," meaning that he insisted that segregated seating come to an end, in the stadium in Mississippi in 1952, or the following year in Chattanooga, Tennessee. I believe he did it in both places. Billy Graham, a son of the Deep South, where Jim Crow laws of purported "separate but equal" were the law of the land, saw things differently. Jim Crow laws resulted in "separate but not equal," and Billy knew it. We have all seen or read stories of the inequities of those laws. At the age of thirty-four Billy was already grasping the inequities, and yet he still had a long way to go to truly see that all lives are equal.

We know he had been influenced by an African American man while still a boy in North Carolina. Reese Brown was the foreman of his father's dairy farm. Billy wrote, "Aside from my father, I admired no one as much as Reese Brown."[112] Brown, a distinguished veteran of World War I, was in charge of all the workers, black, Hispanic, and white. He had great intelligence and was one of Billy's father's best friends. Through Reese, Billy saw that skin color had nothing to do with character and skill. Yet Billy was still a child of the Depression-era American South. Even the landmark Supreme Court ruling of 1954, *Brown vs. the Board of Education*, eliminating segregation in public schools, was yet to be handed down. It wasn't until Billy went to Wheaton College in 1940 that he had fellow students of different colors. This was eye-opening to him. But God would bring many African American leaders into Billy's life, people of theological substance who helped him work through the issue of diversity in his own mind and heart.

As a result, Billy became an advocate for racial healing at a time when even many Christians, sadly, found this unthinkable. In 1952, the United Press quoted Billy in the Jackson, Mississippi, newspaper as saying, "There is no scriptural basis for segregation." However, in the same article, Billy said that while he held that view, he still understood there were social customs that must sometimes be upheld in how public meetings (such as his campaigns and crusades) were held. So while his own view was changing, he was still influenced to some degree by the prevailing prejudice among whites and white institutions. This wouldn't last for long, however. By 1956, Billy was writing in *Life* and *Ebony* magazines that racism is a sin and that he deplored the separation of races in the church.[113]

At the 1957 crusade in New York City, Graham was dedicated and determined to speak against racism. God used two important people to bring him to these settled convictions. The first was a minister from Cleveland, the Reverend Howard O. Jones. Graham invited him to New York to help him and his team understand why so few people of color were coming to the meetings in Madison Square Garden. Jones told Billy to visit the Bronx, Queens, the streets of Harlem, and Brooklyn to listen to the people. Jones showed great patience with Billy and his team while educating them on the injustice and miseries of racism.

Taking Reverend Jones's advice, they held rallies for people of color in Harlem and Brooklyn. Billy was learning. Then, that same year, Jones became an associate evangelist for the Billy Graham Evangelistic Association. His influence on Graham and his team cannot be overemphasized. Most of them were from the South and therefore would need time and understanding to be able to grasp the clear teaching of Scripture on ethnicity apart from their cultural lenses. Billy was, as one of his biographers says, "typically ahead of his own unit, but never at the head of the parade."[114] Howard Olean Jones died in 2010.

The other person God would use to educate Billy on this journey was the famous Reverend Martin Luther King Jr. Leighton Ford, who was heading up communications with churches in New York City in the summer of 1957, remembers that unlike invitations from many other cities, the invitation to come to New York had been offered by the Protestant council of pastors, which included many men of color.

The invitation and the connection with both Martin Luther King Jr. and Clarence B. Jones (King's lawyer and close personal advisor) probably came to Billy by way of these men. Leighton sent a telegram to Dr. King asking if he would be willing to be on the platform and pray an invocational prayer at the beginning of one of the Madison Square Garden events. King agreed, and on July 18, 1957, he and Billy were on a crusade dais together. Over time, a friendship blossomed between the men. Billy would also have Dr. King speak to his executive staff on retreat to educate them more on racial justice. And for his part, it seems that King learned from Billy how to better hold large rallies, and Billy's organizational structures and training were offered to him as well. At one point, the two men wondered if they should even travel together promoting the fullness of the kingdom of God: both changed hearts (the new birth) and changed societies where right replaces wrong. Billy writes:

> Early on, Dr. King and I spoke about his method of using non-violent demonstrations to bring an end to racial segregation. He urged me to keep on doing what I was doing—preaching the gospel to integrated audiences and supporting his goals by example, and not to join him in the streets. "You stay in the stadiums, Billy," he said, "because you will have far more impact on the white establishment there than you would if you marched in the streets. Besides that, you have a constituency that will listen to you, especially among white people, who may not listen so much to me. But if a leader gets too far ahead of his people, they will lose sight of him and not follow him any longer." I followed his advice.[115]

It was also during the New York City crusade of 1957 that President Dwight D. Eisenhower called and asked Billy's advice regarding sending National Guard troops to Little Rock, Arkansas, in order to enforce desegregation laws. Billy's answer was, "I think you've got to, Mr. President. You've got no other alternative. The discrimination must be stopped."[116]

In 1960, Dr. King and Graham were again together, in Brazil for the Baptist World Alliance meetings. During that time, Billy arranged a special dinner for King to meet with US Southern Baptist leaders to try and bridge the chasm between blacks and whites in the American South. "Our friendly relationship with Mike [Dr. King had by this time asked Billy to call him Mike as his other friends did] made the point with my Baptist friends," Billy records in *Just as I Am*.[117] There were, no doubt, times when King wished Billy would be more pronounced and public regarding racial discrimination, and there were probably times when Graham wished King would tone down his rhetoric, going slower on social justice, and preach the new birth in Christ more. Yet the friendship between the men was genuine.

Toward the end of his autobiography, Billy writes of the day he heard Dr. King had died. He was in Australia in the spring of 1968 preaching crusades, but taking an afternoon off to play golf, when journalists ran up and informed him that Dr. King had been shot in Memphis. They asked for a comment. "I was almost in a state of shock," Billy writes. "Not only was I losing a friend through a vicious and senseless killing, but America was losing a social leader and a prophet, and I felt his death would be one of the greatest tragedies in our history. There on the golf course I had all the journalists and the others gathered around, and we bowed in prayer for Dr. King's family, for the United States, and for the healing of the racial divisions of our world. I immediately looked into canceling my schedule and returning for the funeral, but it was impossible because of the great distance."[118] Billy devoted his life to proclaiming the Good News of the changed heart brought about by Jesus Christ in all who love and know him. His own heart, and that of his team, were changed in regard to justice, equality, and racial diversity by special men like Martin Luther King Jr.

In the years to come, Billy's team of associate evangelists traveling the globe to preach Jesus Christ would include Fernando Vangioni from Latin America; Howard O. Jones and Ralph Bell, African Americans; Akbar Abdul-Haqq from Pakistan; and Robert Cunville from India.[119] The commitment to racial justice was so profound for them that Graham would for years refuse to accept invitations to do a crusade in South Africa because of apartheid. Finally, in 1973, he agreed, but only if the crusades were guaranteed to be integrated.[120]

In the United States, before Dr. King's death, the bombing of the church in Birmingham that killed four precious little girls in September 1963 shocked the nation and perhaps as much as any event turned many hearts. Billy was asked to come to Birmingham the following Easter and conduct an integrated meeting calling for people to surrender their hearts to Christ and love one another. It was the largest integrated event in the history of Alabama to that date.[121] His friendship and respect for President Lyndon Johnson also helped Billy go public regarding his support of civil rights. He spoke out in support of the Civil Rights Act of 1964, and the Voting Rights Act of 1965. After "Bloody Sunday" in Selma in March 1965, the president asked him to go to Alabama and hold rallies to support peace and goodwill. He did. And when race riots hit Watts, a neighborhood of Los Angeles, later that year, he flew to California to tour the area with Dr. E. V. Hill, a respected clergyman and confidant of Dr. King, who soon became a member of Billy's board of directors. Billy writes in his autobiography, "I was sickened by the violence and the widespread destruction we saw on every hand. There were no easy answers, I knew, but Dr. Hill and I both agreed that any solution that omitted the need for spiritual renewal could bring only temporary relief."[122] Like us all, Billy Graham was on a journey to learn, to grow, and to repent of his own cultural biases, and he did.

Billy's views on peace and war also sometimes surprised other Christians of his generation and background. In the early years, Billy's political views tended to strongly support American interests and power around the world. Part of the reason for this was fear. The Soviet Union had detonated a nuclear bomb in 1949, and China had become a Communist nation shortly thereafter. World War II ended only four years before these new, frightening events. This was an insecure and shaky time for our nation.

I remember being a small boy in the mid-1950s in Valparaiso, Indiana, and feeling safe. American values permeated our heartland town. Yet even there the threat of thermonuclear war was a topic. In grades three and four my parents, our teachers, and the evening news all spoke of the dangers, which seemed imminent. Wealthy people we knew were building bomb shelters in their homes. My class at school was taught how to get down under our flimsy steel desks and place our heads on the floor in a ducking position in order to protect us from a nuclear blast sure to hit Chicagoland. I saw the mushroom clouds of bomb testings on television.

Graham's relationship, in his early years, with President Dwight D. Eisenhower, the five-star general who engineered D-Day and the final surrender of Germany, probably had something to do with his early worldview. His early sermons were often laced with apocalyptic images of America's fight, and therefore, by extension, God's fight (since he was surely on our side) against Communism. He never stopped preaching and calling for personal conversion to Christ, but he often used the geopolitical dangers in the world to urge listeners to place their trust in the King of kings and to pray for America to be God's hand of goodness and justice in the evil world.

As he aged, he grew in his understandings. I believe it was the trip to Korea in the winter of 1952 to be with US troops fighting in the Korean War that started the change in him. I speak more of this event in the next section, but Billy came back from Korea having seen the carnage and ravage of actual war. He'd not been a soldier in World War II, though he had tried to enlist. Billy wanted to be a chaplain, but his poor health (a dangerous case of the mumps) kept him out. Thus he'd never seen war up close and personal. In the late 1970s he visited one of twentieth century's worst remnants of war: the concentration camps built by Nazi, Germany. He said, "Visits to places like Auschwitz . . . made me reflect long and hard on the hawkish sentiments of my youthful years. I felt that I needed to speak out."[123]

His thorough study of the Bible in all its component parts also allowed him to see that, while apocalyptic disaster is found in the biblical texts, so too is God's deep desire for peace. For instance, the prophets say:

> He will judge between many peoples
> and will settle disputes for strong nations far and wide.
> They will beat their swords into plowshares
> and their spears into pruning hooks.
> Nation will not take up sword against nation,
> nor will they train for war anymore. (Mic. 4:3)

And,

> They will neither harm nor destroy
> on all my holy mountain,
> for the earth will be filled with the knowledge of the LORD
> as the waters cover the sea. (Isa. 11:9)

Graham knew that while only the second coming of Christ would occasion the complete fulfillment of those passages, it was the responsibility of God's kingdom church and people to promote and work for peace until Christ returns. Thus he evolved into a statesman for peace, going to the Soviet Union in 1982, again in 1984, and one more time after the Berlin Wall came down, in 1992. During his 1982 visit, when the Cold War was at its chilliest, he was soundly criticized by the media, certain politicians, and many religious leaders. Even Ruth, his wife, opposed it. But Billy had come to see the nuclear arms race as "insanity and madness."[124] And while his visit to Russia at that time was used by the Kremlin as a promotional ploy, it also slowly opened doors for relationships with leaders that would lead to his preaching the gospel openly to thirty thousand people in Moscow in 1984.[125] Going to Russia in 1982 was one of the most courageous things that Billy Graham ever did. Up to the very night before departure he was unsure he should go. But a decade later, after massive geopolitical changes occurred, Dan Rather, the CBS news anchor and frequent critic of Graham's "fanciful trips," would publicly admit that subsequent events had proved Graham right and his critics wrong.[126] Blessed are the peacemakers.

As I have tried to make abundantly clear, Billy was primarily an evangelist. That was his calling. With every fiber of his being, he spoke the gospel of Jesus Christ to individuals the world over, telling of God's love and the need to repent of sin and enter a never-ending relationship with him. However, as he aged he also realized that, while the need for Christ is chronic for all humankind, there is also an acute need to alleviate human suffering and need. One is chronic, the other acute; both are necessary. He would always focus on the need for personal salvation, but not to the exclusion of loving our neighbors as ourselves.

As early as 1950, while in his early thirties, Billy became friends with Bob Pierce, who had started an organization called World Vision. Pierce's famous quote was, "Let my heart be broken with the things that break the heart of God." Pierce would tell Graham about the extent of human suffering the world over. Billy had Bob preach one of the crusade nights in Portland in 1950 to share his passions with a larger audience.[127] Bob then invited Billy to travel with him to see the extent of the sorrows. In 1952, the two men, along with Grady Wilson, received special permission from the US government to travel to Korea to visit our troops and see the devastation of that land in the midst of ravaging war and poverty. Billy witnessed human suffering at that time, which was beyond any of his previous experiences. Grady later remarked that Korea was a turning point for Billy. From that time on, he preached with more compassion for people and their daily needs. Billy said on one *Hour of Decision* broadcast one day, soon after their return from Korea, "Our hearts were rent and torn at what we've seen and heard."[128] The poverty and misery of war in Korea started to change him and set him on a slow but deliberate course to advocate and take action to alleviate human suffering by standing alongside and promoting organizations such as World Vision.

He then utilized his evangelistic organization to be more involved as well. In the late 1960s and early '70s, the BGEA formed a special fund to bring humanitarian aid to places facing natural disasters and other emergencies. It was officially called the World Emergency Fund. Two events galvanized Graham's commitment to this task. First was the Guatemala earthquake of 1976. Billy and Ruth were in Mexico, where Ruth was recovering from an illness, when they heard of the crisis and arranged to have aid flown in from the United States. Billy, Ruth, and Cliff Barrows flew in ahead of the helicopters, landing in the city of San Martín Jilotepeque. Every building had been destroyed. Of the eighteen thousand residents who lived there, nearly four thousand had perished suddenly. Another four thousand were wounded, but there was no medical help. Graham wrote that he and Ruth felt totally helpless as they watched thousands wandering about in a daze looking for food or lost relatives.[129]

The second tipping-point event occurred in 1977, when the BGEA team was in India for crusades. A massive cyclone and tidal wave hit the state of Andhra Pradesh while they were there. The waves were eighteen feet high and fifty miles wide. Hundreds of villages were destroyed. More than 100,000 people perished. Billy and many members of his team flew into the affected area to see the devastation for themselves and figure out what they could do in response. The World Emergency Fund then provided for many necessities, helping to rebuild one village, including a local church; this became a model for the rebuilding of other villages.[130]

While the Graham organization had a heart for compassion, in actuality they had little expertise in handling these emergency situations. They were not a relief organization. Therefore, they began partnering with excellent Christian relief organizations already in place. What the BGEA realized they could do best was advocate for aid, providing dollars from their own funds, and call for Christians the world over to support these great agencies. I saw this in action at the thirteen crusades and numerous festivals I attended with Billy and his son Franklin. At each, local churches would work with the BGEA to determine what relief and development projects were most needed in their city or country. Canned foods were donated, and backpacks with pencils and paper for underserved children to go to school were collected. All manner of help was provided. And when one remembers that between 100,000 and 250,000 people attended the typical crusade, donations could make a great dent in a great need. It always lifted my spirit to see these things in action.

Finally, let me add: When Billy visited places of great need, simply visiting with the people and praying for them, this awakened the world to the need. That was the reality of his fame and influence, and how God used him. Media followed him everywhere too, and posted stories of what he said and what he saw. I recall, for instance, the San Francisco earthquake of October 1989. I had been a pastor in the area until earlier that summer, when we moved to the Chicago suburbs. My old church and its people were part of the catastrophe in the Bay Area, and I had a strong sense of survivor's guilt, and wished I could be with them to help. But within a day or so Billy arrived. One of my pastor friends led him as part of a welcoming team of clergy to the devastation, including the collapse of a portion of the Bay Bridge. There he was again, going to where the need was, and the media followed him like hawks. What they televised was Billy with the people; "America's Pastor" had come. It makes me weep now to think of it. I remember watching him on TV from our home in Chicago. He cared, he prayed. His agency helped, and his informal leadership of the evangelical movement would come to help too. I didn't know him personally then. It would be another ten years before I would join the team in my limited way. I never thanked him for going to San Francisco when I could not go myself. In some ways, he pastored me those days as well.

This arena of alleviating human suffering was not an ordered part of his early career. As I noted earlier, he focused on the vertical relationship with God while supporting other agencies devoted to the horizontal needs of people on earth. But as with his approach to racial justice, he grew. Today the BGEA works closely with one of the largest and most effective relief agencies in the world, Samaritan's Purse. The same man who influenced Billy toward good works, Bob Pierce, the founder of World Vision, would mentor Billy's son, Franklin, in this work. Samaritan's Purse exists to give physical aid to victims of war, natural disasters, disease, famine, poverty, and persecution in more than one hundred countries. They work closely with Christian churches wherever they are. Franklin has grown the agency until today, it is a $600-million-per-year global relief entity. It received a four-star rating—the highest—from the watchdog agency Charity Navigator for effective use of funds to accomplish the most good.[131] Franklin serves as president and CEO.

Franklin also became his father's successor as the president and CEO of the BGEA at the start of the twenty-first century. Today, the two organizations are devoted to "Evangelism Always" (the vision of BGEA) and "to provide spiritual and physical aid to hurting people around the world" (the vision of Samaritan's Purse). I have had the privilege of watching Franklin and his teams in both organizations. They are passionate, committed, and effective. Franklin is a gifted evangelist and a godly pastor to a world in need. In a sense, the son has taken the father's values to a new level, and the world is a lot better because of it.

I will always remember the time when Franklin invited me to visit him at Samaritan's Purse headquarters in Boone, North Carolina. That same day, a hurricane was in the waters off the coast of Florida with a projected landing somewhere on Florida's east coast or as far up as the Outer Banks of North Carolina. On the tarmac below the Samaritan's Purse offices were two semis being loaded with relief supplies, engines running. He told me to go look at the trucks. Generators, food, clothing, and water filled the trailers. As soon as that hurricane hit, the trucks would hit the road. That's Samaritan's Purse.

In all these things, from Billy Graham's early years in ministry up to his death, and now among his family and friends, his work continues, and one can see the Christian doctrine of the kingdom of God at work. God's kingdom rules and reigns on earth now, and will rule and reign someday soon completely and forever. Both aspects of the kingdom became clear guidelines to Graham's commitments to make the world better and to save souls. I ask you, dear reader: Do you have hope for a better world and future? Coming to personal faith in Jesus Christ does more than meet your personal needs and fears; it transforms you into one of God's kingdom operatives, making right whatever is wrong. Consider Christ. Join your life to his and become more than you imagined you would ever be.

EIGHT
WEAKNESSES
AND REGRETS

For we do not have a high priest [Jesus Christ] who is unable to empathize with our weaknesses, but we have one who has been tempted in every way, just as we are—yet he did not sin. Let us then approach God's throne of grace with confidence, so that we may receive mercy and find grace to help us in our time of need.

—Hebrews 4:15–16

———

Although I have much to be grateful for as I look back over my life, I also have many regrets. I have failed many times, and I would do many things differently.

—BILLY GRAHAM[132]

I need to write this chapter to save myself. I told you in the beginning that Billy disliked books about him for fear people would start to idolize or focus on him rather than the Jesus who made him. I vowed to avoid making him too much of a hero. But I'm afraid I may have done so. What is it in me and in us that wants human heroes? Whatever it is, this chapter is meant to be a corrective. No one was harder on Billy than Billy. So here we go, exposing the "chinks in his armor."

I keep humming the line from the old Frank Sinatra song "I Did It My Way," where he sings, "Regrets, I have a few, but then again too few to mention." Billy was not Frank, but often in his writings and speeches Billy spoke of his weaknesses and failures as if they were many. He begins his nearly eight-hundred-page autobiography by telling the story of one big failure in his life. His youthful pomposity in 1950 (he was only thirty-one) led him and his team to abuse the privilege of seeing President Truman by telling the press afterward things they should have kept to themselves.[133] He also devoted several pages at the end to chronicling regrets and weaknesses.

This may sound odd to some, but I believe that exposing our weaknesses as Christians helps us. It saves us from pride and saves others from ever thinking we are the source of our occasional goodness. We believe our goodness, whenever it is manifest, is all God from beginning to end. The apostle Paul, when writing about the amazing transformation that takes place in a soul when it is linked with Christ, stops almost mid-sentence and quickly inserts, "but we ourselves are like fragile clay jars containing this great treasure. This makes it clear that our great power is from God, not from ourselves" (2 Cor. 4:6–7). Someone once said that God places his beauty and goodness in human "cracked pots." I like that. It sure fits me.

Before we discuss Graham's regrets and weaknesses, however, I want to write about some steps he and his team took early in their careers to guard one another from sin and its consequences. In October 1948, they were in Modesto, California, conducting a small and not very successful series of meetings. Billy was twenty-nine years old. This was a full year before the Los Angeles breakthrough and their being catapulted into the spotlight. Billy called his small traveling team together to discuss issues of character and accountability. Cliff Barrows, George Beverly

Shea, and Grady Wilson were there. Nothing was wrong, necessarily, but the more they traveled the more they realized that evangelists had a bad reputation in America. Some of it was earned. Too many evangelists operated independently, with no checks and balances to their behavior or fidelity in their organizations. I am sure most of them were upstanding people with godly motives, but not all were.

As I discussed in a previous chapter, *Elmer Gantry*, written in 1927 by American novelist Sinclair Lewis about a corrupt evangelist, was so influential that the term "Elmer Gantry" came to describe Christian evangelism not only for that era but also decades later. I still hear it used occasionally as a derogatory term. The book was made into a feature film in 1960 with the flamboyant Burt Lancaster playing the title role, for which he received an Academy Award for Best Actor. That didn't help much either.

Billy drew his team together and asked that each person take an hour and write out a list of the problems that plagued the integrity of evangelistic campaigns. They each went to their rooms in the old-fashioned Hotel Modesto and listed the most frequent criticisms. They came back together with lists of ten to fifteen common factors, which they narrowed to four key aspects of Christian character.[134] These have become known as the "Modesto Manifesto" in Billy Graham circles. They are:

1. *Shady handling of money.* At that time nearly every evangelist received his income through offerings at meetings. These appeals for contributions could easily become drawn out and emotionally conniving. Billy started that way as well. But soon they set up an organization with a board of directors that would set salaries

for the employees. Offerings would be taken at the meetings, but the amount received had no influence on how much each team member received. Later, Graham would help organize the Evangelical Council for Financial Accountability, which for decades has provided prudent concepts of fiscal propriety for hundreds of organizations.

2. *Sexual immorality.* They all knew of men who had fallen sexually and yet continued in their up-front ministries. They also knew that this was a problem that had to be avoided at all costs. Perceptions are everything, and I presume that as young, vibrant, handsome men, they too had to struggle against this temptation. I've been a pastor and evangelist for more than forty-five years myself, and I have met few in my calling who have not struggled in this area, including me. The Bible says, "Flee also youthful lusts" (2 Tim. 2:22 KJV). That's good counsel. The team made a commitment to each other that each one would never be alone with a woman who was not his wife. That is stringent. They were accountable to each other in this area. Today, the "Modesto Manifesto" in this area of sexual morality is known even in the US government. Early in 2017, Vice President Mike Pence made headlines when he told the media that he long ago had adopted this policy in his life. He was roundly criticized in Washington, DC, and beyond. This seemed archaic to many. I realize this principle seems severe and in some ways can hinder friendship between men and women, but it is possible to adopt it and still find ways to allow healthy interactions between men and women that bless everyone.

3. *Badmouthing others doing similar work.* Our tongues can be dangerous or beautiful depending on what we use them to say. We all know how easy it is to backstab, slander, and cause factions with words. Evidently, in Billy's early days evangelists often disrespected the local church and hardworking pastors. Some used a criticizing spirit to draw larger crowds. Billy's team knew this was wrong and set in stone to always cooperate with the local church and other Christian enterprises. They held each other accountable to not badmouth others. I once found a good quotation of Cliff Barrows reflecting on Graham twenty years after this principle was set: "I've never once heard him publicly say one derogatory remark about any minister. . . . He always held up the clergy in the highest esteem before the people."[135]

4. *Exaggerate accomplishments.* In Billy's early days, it was tempting to exaggerate successes, hyperbolize results, in order to convince donors to keep supporting the work, or cities to invite you to come. One of the first things Billy and his colleagues did was to report people making some kind of spiritual decision as "inquirers," not converts. Using good biblical theology, they said that only God knows when someone is converted or born again. Therefore, all who responded at the meetings who were willing were gently counseled as inquirers, knowing that time would tell if a lasting life change had occurred. Attendance figures is another area where exaggeration could find a foothold. The Graham team policy is to count attendees, but also allow the venue and sometimes the city to make their own separate counts. The counts are then compared, and the organization reports the smallest of

the numbers as official. This is an issue of integrity to them, and I watched them hold to this policy to the letter in my fifteen years of going to the big meetings.

This briefly summarizes the essential principles of the "Modesto Manifesto." Though these commitments were forged some seventy years ago, they are just as relevant today. Why? Because we are talking about character. These things are about money, sex, power, and the inherent dangers in what we say about others. Think how much better our world would be if generosity replaced greed, fidelity replaced immorality, serving replaced power grabbing, and our tongues blessed more than cursed. In every generation we see what happens when men and women fall to these temptations. One of the promises from the Bible that led me to consider becoming a Christian was God's promise to help us say no to sin and poor character and become a better person. It says, "No temptation has overtaken you except what is common to mankind. And God is faithful; he will not let you be tempted beyond what you can bear. But when you are tempted, he will also provide a way out so that you can endure it" (1 Cor. 10:13). I've seen God be faithful to help me in this area of character for forty-five years. I am a long way from perfect, but a lot better than I used to be.

Manifesto or not, Billy wanted to be pure and authentic before God and the people he served. He understood the need to know what was right and what was wrong, and knew how important it was to have people of godly character around him to hold him accountable. If there is one tenet that runs throughout the gospel, it is that we are all sinners desperately in need of God's help to become what we are meant to be.

Still, Billy made mistakes. Toward the end of his public life, at the age of eighty, he wrote about the regrets and weaknesses that slipped through.

1. "I would speak less and study more."[136]

This was a repeated theme throughout his later life reflections. He said the same thing to Greta Susteren of Fox News in his last public interview, in 2010. He was, as we wrote earlier, an avid learner with insatiable curiosity. He wished he had studied more. Several of his projects were to provide graduate-level theological learning to others that he himself never received. He built the Billy Graham Center at Wheaton College to provide a quality learning atmosphere for the Wheaton Graduate School and to start a worldwide hub of programs and projects for higher learning in all fields related to the expansion of Christianity. When I directed the Graham Center and would occasionally visit him, I was always asked to give him an update on the graduate school. He was joyful to receive reports of men and women from around the world coming to study Jesus Christ and his mission to the world. He also helped start Gordon-Conwell Theological Seminary near Boston for the same purposes. Gordon-Conwell has become one of the premier seminaries in the world.

But would he really have wished to speak less? When asked further about that comment with Greta, he said that he meant *speak less in smaller settings*. He didn't mean the crusades. He meant the thousands of other functions in the cities he traveled to. Those events sapped his energies. Many if not most of them could have been given to his associates, allowing him more time for reading and dialogue with scholars who were readily available to engage with him at any time and help advance his learning about God and Jesus Christ.

2. "I am staggered by all the things we did and the engagements we kept."[137]

He was not bragging as he writes those words. He was, in fact, lamenting. A lot of life was lost traveling, continually "flitting" (his word, not mine) from place to place. He questioned his discernment to have been as incessantly busy and driven as he was. Of course, his own lifestyle pattern rubbed off on all his team as well. We admire hard work, long hours, endless deadlines in our culture. This pattern is exacerbated to near addiction for people in professional ministry. We consider the work we do so vital for the good of the world and the message of Jesus so essential for life now and forever that we can become slaves to it. Graham's people are some of the most hardworking people I have ever known. This weakness afflicts me continually as well. I am comfortable with the term "workaholic" to categorize Billy, his team, and myself.

I once had lunch with Cliff Barrows and his wife, Ann, in a lovely restaurant in Atlanta near their home. Somehow, the issue of retirement came up. By this time, Cliff was in his eighties. I may have brought up the subject and asked if there were policies for retirement age in the Graham association. I remember Cliff sitting back, reminiscing, and saying something like, "Lon, we just never thought about retirement. Our work was never-ending and expanding and we just didn't talk much about when we might slow down." From that luncheon, I deduced that the Graham founding team would retire when they expired! That's pretty much what has happened. They all died still employed, as far as I know.

I saw this practice lived out through T. W. Wilson too, one of Billy's boyhood friends and coworkers for life. T. W. was a master administrator and sometimes protector of Billy in the early days. He was built like a bodyguard. When I knew him, he was Graham's chief of staff in Montreat. Late in his life, he was a member of the Billy Graham Center advisory committee and faithfully flew to Chicago three times a year to meet with me and my team. I enjoyed his wit and his beautiful spirit. At the last meeting he attended, he was not feeling well. David Bruce and Sterling Huston made sure he got back to the hotel after that Friday-morning meeting to rest. He did, and then flew home on Saturday. On Monday morning, T. W. went to the office, cleaned out his desk, and told David Bruce he was just too old to carry out his duties and that David should take over for the present. He said goodbye to the staff. His wife drove him home. That Thursday, while his wife was driving him somewhere, T. W. leaned his head against the window glass, closed his eyes, and went to heaven. He retired when he expired.

3. *"Every day I was absent from my family is gone forever."*[138] What a penetrating quotation. The workaholism led to the greater weakness, or sin if you will, of placing family second, third, fourth, or fifth to the work. In his writings, Billy always gushed over his wife, Ruth, for many reasons. One of her great strengths was her capacity to raise the children while he was absent. He was usually absent. Yet he loved his family deeply. He and Ruth had five great kids. All of them have children and grandchildren now. Billy often could not remember

how many grandchildren and great-grandchildren he had. It's a lot. Even in my brief meetings with him, our conversations almost always started by talking about each other's families. In those later years, when he was in his eighties and beyond, he was starting to slow down due to physical afflictions. Those years gave him time to reflect and, I believe, regret a lot. "Every day I was absent from my family is gone forever."

I remember a rather humorous moment when I first went to work with the BGEA and Wheaton College. I had been asked to fly from Chicago to Los Angeles to attend Billy's board meetings and give a brief update on the work of the Graham Center. They wanted me to share my vision for its work. We started the meetings with an opening dinner around tables, where conversation and friendship can flourish. I was placed at Cliff Barrows's table, something that was always a joy. Cliff was one of the most gracious and friendly humans on the planet. I felt immediately received and welcomed as "a part of them all." Billy's table was across the room, but I could still see him there being gracious with his tablemates. Up until this point, I had only met him for the interview in Ottawa.

Most of us went to our rooms soon after the dinner. I was especially weary. After all, I had flown all day, and "back in time" from Chicago to Los Angeles, so I was dealing with jet lag and time loss. I was also nervous about my presentation to be given the next morning. I fell fast asleep by 9:00 PM West Coast time, but then, just before 10:00, the phone rang in my room. I woke in a stupor, and fearfully. I had been traveling often for many years and, from experience, I knew that when the phone rang at this time of night it almost always meant there was a problem at home. I answered. It was a man's voice on the other end of the line, not that of my wife, Marie.

"Is this Lon Allison?" he said.

"Yes," I responded. "Who is this?"

"Bill," said the voice.

"Bill who?" I said, still with a tone of annoyance. Then I slowly began to wake, as the voice began to sound all too familiar in my waking brain.

"Billy Graham."

I sat up straight in bed, and for the next ten or fifteen minutes we talked. Billy thanked me for making the trip to join his meeting. I felt I should be thanking him. Then he talked about his family. He asked about mine and said jokingly, "Lon, I have a lot of problems." "You do, sir," I replied, not yet knowing how to address him. "Yes, and it's because of my family," he added. Pause. He went on. "First of all, we had too many children." Now I knew he was joking, and indeed he was. The conversation then focused solely on telling good stories to each other of our wives, and our children whom we loved. I don't know that I ever felt as close to him as that night on the phone. And I could feel his love and concern for his loved ones.

Billy says in *Just as I Am* that as he aged he sought forgiveness from the children for his absence. I think he also felt the same about being away from his beloved Ruth so often for so long. Workaholism can rob us and those we love of precious life and family moments together. This was probably his greatest regret and weakness. Mine too. I am sixty-five, and I have cancer. And yet I feel guilty when I'm not working all the time. When I am working, I feel I am fulfilling my calling. I don't actually know if Billy had this affliction as bad as I have, but may God save us from it. Selah.

4. "I would also spend more time in spiritual nurture,
seeking to grow closer to God."[139]

This regret surprised me when I first heard it. A whole chapter in this book is on the strength of Billy's personal life with God, and yet here he regrets not being closer to God. Maybe that is because once a person meets Christ and draws near to the Father through him, he wants more and more of that fellowship. King David wrote in the Psalms,

> You, God, are my God,
>
> earnestly I seek you;
>
> I thirst for you,
>
> my whole being longs for you. (Ps. 63:1)

Graham longed for God more and more.

He also said he wished he could pray and read the Scriptures without always using that time to prepare for the next sermon or speech. That is a telling statement. I again can relate. Presently, I speak or teach about once a week somewhere in my own wonderful church called Wheaton Bible, or in conferences or other churches or theological schools. It's hard for me to just be with God to be with God. I always have an ulterior motive, and that is, *What am I going to say at my next assignment?* Once you start preaching, a part of your brain is on permanent alert to gather information to feed out to others. Well, imagine what this was like for Billy Graham! He must have spoken on average five times or more a week for six decades. He must have always been in prep mode. When that is the case we are in danger of "using God" for our work more than merely being with him, which is our joy.

5. "And I would give more attention to fellowship with other Christians."[140]

This goes back to the busyness problem. I believe Billy wished he had taken more time to have close friends and mentors, and to be a mentor to others in smaller settings. It is one of the great joys of life to have close friends who walk alongside you on the journey. I don't know how personally close he was to his team and how often they were able to leave the work behind and talk of poems and prayers and promises and things that we believe in (apologies to John Denver!). I'm sad for him that it appears he loved people and had friends but that his incessantly busy life robbed him of more.

6. "If I had it to do over again, I would also avoid any semblance of involvement in partisan politics."[141]

This weakness is the one most commented on by historians. As we have already seen, Billy had personal relationships with eleven sitting US presidents. He also had friendships with the queen of England, Winston Churchill, and many other foreign leaders. His calling as an evangelist and pastor was to provide spiritual counsel to people in power when needed. But it is very clear that in his early years he advocated and voiced his opinions on a number of political, governing, and election issues. He allowed his position of influence to gather voters for certain leaders, even if he did not publicly endorse them. All it would take was a picture with a leader to suggest support. How many votes John F. Kennedy garnered by simply riding in a convertible with Billy can never be measured. Later in life he ended such behavior and sought to be only a spiritual guide to people of power. But he learned the hard way. It had to do with Richard Nixon.

One of the most sobering periods of Billy's life was his personal relationship with President Richard M. Nixon. He devotes a full twenty pages to it in his autobiography. They were clearly close friends. Graham describes Nixon as caring, sincere, spiritual, and of course, brilliant. He also thought of him as a highly moral man. He did see signs of brokenness and sadness, however. Nixon had grown up a Quaker, and his mother had a close relationship with Jesus. He was quiet about his faith, and Graham thought it to be genuine and believing, at least most of the time. Over forty years of friendship, Billy was sometimes left wondering if Nixon's faith was real. He asked him several times to make sure his heart was right with God. He cared deeply for Nixon and his family and wanted him to find the peace that comes from knowing God.

When the Watergate scandal first broke, Billy hoped it would be "a brief parenthesis or blip in a good man's lengthy political career."[142] But then when the Watergate tapes were released and Billy heard the president's language and tone he was deeply distressed. He said, "I felt physically sick and went into the seclusion of my study at the back of the house. Inwardly I felt torn apart. . . . I wanted to believe the best about him for as long as I could. When the worst came out, it was nearly unbearable for me."[143] The friendship was wounded, but would not end. Billy would end up caring for the family and eventually leading President Nixon's memorial service in 1994.

The tragedy was not over, however, for Billy with Nixon's death. He was soon to confront an even deeper sorrow and face a dark side of his own soul, exposing deeper chinks in his reputation. In 2002, the National Archives released many of the White House tapes that had been recorded under Nixon's authority. One of them was a conversation between President Nixon, his chief of staff, and Billy Graham. The president was voicing anti-Semitic remarks about media elites and his view that they controlled much of the immoral material being shown on television and other venues. Billy was caught up in the conversation, and expressed some of his own bias on the same issue. It is hard to listen to. It went viral. Upon hearing it, Billy was himself shocked about what he had said. Yet he also made no attempts to excuse it or explain it away. To get more of this story, read historian Grant Wacker's treatment in *America's Pastor*.[144] Americans expected better things from Billy, and he did too. He apologized publicly and over the next few years sought personal forgiveness from Jewish friends he had offended.

What was behind this event? What happened to Billy Graham? He sinned. The Bible says, "There is no one righteous, not even one" (Rom. 3:10). In a revised version of his autobiography from 2007, Billy got very honest about his own areas of brokenness. He admitted that a sense of condemnation for his sins had plagued him most of his life. He struggled with feeling unworthy. He said,

> I asked the Lord to help me, and it seemed to me that there was a big screen, and on it appeared a list of all my sins going back to childhood. Then all of a sudden, under them appeared a verse of Scripture: "The blood of Jesus Christ his Son cleanseth us from all sin" (1 John 1:7, KJV) and I had a great peace that has not left me to this day. Since then I have met everything that might have become a crisis with peace, certain that God is in control. Slowly but surely the feelings of condemnation left me.[145]

It must be hard to keep one's head and one's God perspective when you are at every turn sought by the masses and the rich, the powerful, and the famous. But in all his weaknesses and sins it was always Billy's hope that people would think less of him and more of Jesus, who was without sin and who forgives all our sins if we but seek him.

I often use the following illustration as I explain the majesty of God's forgiveness of his people. It is called the "goodness scale" analogy. I ask a listener to consider, on a scale of one to ten, where would they put themselves on the goodness scale. A one or two would be like a Hitler or a terrorist. A ten would be a Mother Teresa or a Billy Graham. But I now add (I learned this from a wonderful pastor, Bill Hybels) that, before they answer, I need them to know that neither Billy nor Mother Teresa saw themselves as a ten, but more like a three or four. In other words, the best among us see ourselves as severely flawed on the goodness scale. The Bible says you have to be a ten to get right with God for now and eternity (see Matt. 5:48 and Jas. 2:10). We must be a ten. How? We can't, of course. Only one person was: Jesus Christ. His perfection and loving sacrifice of his own life for our sins can make us a ten in God's eyes. Jesus was perfect, not me, not you, and not Billy Graham. Do you see more clearly now why Billy always wanted people to know Jesus more than him?

NINE

A SOUL MATE
FOR LIFE

Two are better than one,
because they have a good return for their labor:
If either of them falls down,
one can help the other up.
But pity anyone who falls
and has no one to help them up.
Also, if two lie down together, they will keep warm.
But how can one keep warm alone?
Though one may be overpowered,
two can defend themselves.
—*Ecclesiastes 4:9–12*

Ruth is my soul mate and best friend and I cannot imagine living a single day without her by my side. I am more and more in love with her today than when we first met 65 years ago.

— BILLY GRAHAM[146]

The Billy Graham story is also the story of his beloved wife and best friend, Ruth. They were married nearly sixty-four years. It is a love story and a life story of God's goodness and provision. Billy once said, "Ruth and I don't have the perfect marriage, but we have a great one."[147] They were very different people, according to Ruth:

> Bill's and my tastes differ in books, music, style, décor, food, hobbies and so forth. Even our forms of relaxing differ. I go for a good book. He, immersed in books most of the time as it is, used to play golf, now walks. Our temperaments differ. By nature I am easygoing to the point of laziness, and am basically optimistic. Bill is highly disciplined and drives himself unmercifully.[148]

Both were expressive, verbal people. Ruth was known for her quick wit, humor, and poet's eye and voice. Billy was known for his straight-forward, clear, and direct speech. Both loved Jesus and bathed in the Scriptures as a daily part of life. Thus they shared similar and deeply held values about God, family, and the purpose for living. These values were the glue that allowed two different personalities to flourish in life together.

Early in their lives before the children were born she would sometimes travel with him on campaigns and crusades. In her inimitable way she said, "I cannot keep up with the man. In fact, taking me on a crusade is rather like a general taking his wife to battle with him. Our happiest times together are at home or on vacation (though he usually takes his vacations like the drivers of the Indianapolis 500 take their pit stops—as seldom and as quickly as possible)."[149]

There was never any doubt about their affection for one another or for their five children. And the kids knew how much Dad loved Mom and vice versa. Sometimes they would "smooch" right out in the open. The children remember that Dad would sometimes sneak up to his wife, guide her away from her kitchen duties, and waltz her around the room. Throughout the day, he held her hand or sat her in his lap, the two of them laughing and teasing as if romance was fresh like springtime. "His love and tenderness toward her were something we daughters looked for in our husbands," their youngest daughter, Bunny, wrote.[150]

The young family first lived in Montreat, just off a primary two-lane road. Unfortunately, that road was readily accessible to people wanting to see Billy Graham, and that could present problems. Those were difficult times. Between well-wishers, religious "kooks," the press, and sometimes even threatening people, the family was in a fish bowl until 1956. By that time, four of the children were born and the family home was becoming too small. An opportunity came to buy a relatively large tract of land only a mile away. It was off the beaten track, up a hill, and would offer more privacy. Billy and Ruth purchased two hundred acres that was mostly hills and therefore unbuildable, for just thirteen dollars per acre. The property had a nice, flat area on top of one of the hills. Soon, they had a road put in to drive up the steep side of the hills. Ruth began planning a modest North Carolina ranch-style home. She looked for authentic North Carolina materials and expressed her creativity and personality in every part of the design and its furnishings. She especially liked fireplaces and convinced Billy to have not one but two in their new house. Then, once he left for India on a crusade, she convinced the builders to put in a total of five fireplaces![151]

Most of the first phase was built in 1956. This allowed the family room to grow, and most importantly, a place to be safe and enjoy family life. It was never, and still is not, an ostentatious home in any way. The

Graham home feels like a welcoming place in the rugged mountains. When you walk in, you usually come in through the door leading to the kitchen, and right away a visitor has the sense of being welcomed as family. I think that is exactly what Ruth hoped to express. Soon, her parents moved in just down the road. In 1957, after the home was built, Billy was able to spend that entire spring off the road as he prepared for the big, upcoming crusade in New York City. I know that that spring was one of Billy's most enjoyable times of life. He was with Ruth and his precious children nearly every day, day after day.

But life was difficult for the Grahams too. Billy's growing world ministry called him away for a tremendous part of their lives together. Billy traveled up to six months a year.[152] This left Ruth as the primary parent raising a family of five children. Her parents assisted in every way they could, but it was hard.

Both Billy and Ruth suffered loneliness apart from each other. He tried to call every night, but a telephone connection is a far cry from being with one another. One of Ruth's poems expressed this far better than I can:

We live a time
Secure;
Sure
It cannot last
For long
Then
The goodbyes come
Again again
Like a small death,

The closing of a door.
One learns to live
With pain.
One looks ahead,
Not back,
. . . never back,
Only before.
And joy will come again
Warm and secure,
If only for the now,
Laughing,
We endure.[153]

I doubt one can ever get used to loneliness. Ruth's pattern was to be strong and immediately get new projects going or activities with the kids and, as she says, never look back but only ahead. Perhaps that helped dull the sense of loss. I hope, too, that it enabled Ruth to draw near to Jesus, who said, "Never will I leave you; never will I forsake you" (Heb. 13:5). It was hard on Billy as well. "Many a time, I've driven down that driveway with tears coming down my cheeks, not wanting to leave," he said.[154]

The children missed their daddy, and he missed them terribly. Their firstborn, Gigi, remembers one time when her daddy was disciplining her for bad behavior. As she was being spanked she cried, "Some father you are! You go away and leave us alone all the time." She says he stopped and suddenly his eyes filled with tears.[155] Another time, Billy remembers hearing his little boy Franklin's voice calling out as he departed, "Daddy, don't go."[156]

The time of separation and single parenting forced Ruth to live several roles at once, including that of disciplinarian. It wasn't easy, and because of the family notoriety, when one of the children would get in trouble, it would often be publicized. She lamented, "None of our children can ever live privately, conquer privately, or sin privately."[157]

Every family is perfectly imperfect. The Grahams were no different. There is no doubt the children sacrificed a lot to have their father gone so much. Other families, including yours and mine, bear the brunt of sorrows and imperfection as well. Some have greater challenges than others. I think of single-parent families in my congregation. Or families with severe illness affecting a child. I think of those kids in my congregation who are foster children hoping for a surrogate parent who mighty really love them. I think of grieving families in Chicago, where the murder rate of teens and young adults is so high in parts of the city. How do such families cope? I believe all adults carry some wounds and/or scars from imperfect upbringings, some more than others.

I doubt that the Graham children think their lot was any worse than that of most families. I honestly don't know. I have watched them from a distance. All five of them appear to have lives of importance and purpose. I know there are stories of dissension in the family. And because at least two of the children have high profiles in the Christian world, they are watched and critiqued more than most of us ever will be. I once heard that when it comes to criticism, the winds always blow harder when you are at the top of the tree.

Billy carried a lot of regret about his years away from the family, as we saw in the last chapter. But he also experienced God's forgiveness and was given many years to make amends. I believe this did happen, and that it was their "family business." They deserve our prayers as they each process it with God's guidance.

The truth is that there is a longing in every person to have a healthy and whole family system. But the truth is, no human family achieves anywhere close to perfection in this area. Once again, I turn to the Christian message of the gospel to find comfort and understanding. Jesus tells those who love him to call God Father. If you've ever heard or prayed the Lord's Prayer, taught to the world by Jesus, you know it begins with Jesus saying, pray like this: "Our Father . . ." (Matt. 6:9). God desires his people to imagine him as a good and loving Father. This is family language, and God wants us to experience authentic and whole family in our relationship with him and his people. In several places in the New Testament, all who know and love God are encouraged to see themselves as part of his household. I like this verse: "So now you Gentiles [meaning, non-Jews who didn't know God personally, but now do] are no longer strangers and foreigners. . . . You are members of God's family" (Eph. 2:19 NLT).

God wants you to be part of his family. He is the perfect parent and is always available to be with you in every life moment. Further, when we receive him as Father we also become part of his worldwide family, called the church. We are encouraged to think of fellow believers in Jesus as brothers and sisters. I am so thankful for so many brothers and sisters. What I am trying to say is that becoming a believer in Jesus Christ makes you part of God the Father's own family. There is comfort in that, and hope. And remember, you can't earn adoption into this family. But God offers it freely if you turn your life over to him. This verse says it a lot better than I can: "Yet to all who did receive him, to those who believed in his name, he gave the right to become children of God" (Jn. 1:12). What a promise!

In 1974, Ruth's health took a nosedive. By then, all the children were out of the home and Ruth was spending much of her time with the grandkids. She was a natural grandmother, full of playfulness and joy. One day while visiting Gigi in Wisconsin, with her typical spunk and can-do attitude she decided to build a pipe slide for the grandchildren. She fastened wire between two trees at a sharp angle and then put the pipe around it to slide back and forth. The children would be able to grip the pipe and go sliding over the yard between the trees. She decided to test it before allowing the kids to try it. The wire snapped and she plummeted fifteen feet, striking the ground hard enough to injure her foot as well as her head. And that wasn't all. A quick trip to the emergency room revealed that Ruth had a broken rib, a shattered heel, a crushed vertebra, and a severe brain concussion. She was in a coma for a week.

At age fifty-four, Ruth suffered a terrible trauma on her body that would result in long-term painful degenerative arthritis in her neck and back. Eventually, she would require a morphine pump to deal with pain. As time went on, other physical afflictions occurred as well.[158] She would struggle with chronic pain the rest of her life.

It was also near the time of the accident that both of her parents died. Ruth's father, Dr. L. Nelson Bell, passed in 1973, and her mother, Virginia McCue Bell, in 1974.[159] The children were grown up and living elsewhere, Billy's work continued to call him away, and her parents were gone.

She wouldn't allow the pain and loneliness to control her life. She traveled with Billy some of the time, usually for shorter trips, and gave love and care to the always-growing family. She prayed for them, spoke and visited with them, and even wrote books and poetry following her accident. She would continue to serve Jesus and love him for thirty-three more years.

Billy's final public crusade was held in 2005. His own health had been severely challenged in numerous ways, and he had been slowing down for a few years. Once that last crusade was over, Ruth and Billy were like two aging saints limited by time and affliction. Both of them loved their mountain home, and now for the first time in their lives they could be with one another in their beloved mountains continually. Billy's eyesight and hearing for the most part left him in the years that followed. Other maladies afflicted him as well. But that didn't slow or in any way diminish the love story of this remarkable couple. Every day, I am told, Billy would be at Ruth's bedside, talking, remembering, praying, and sitting contentedly together in silence. Then, on June 14, 2007, Ruth Bell Graham departed this world for the next. On her gravestone at the Billy Graham Library in Charlotte is a headstone that reads, "Construction ended. Thanks for your patience." Her charm and personality were in full force until the very end. But Billy was then alone.

Billy Graham's life journey concluded on February 21, 2018. We believe he entered a final and blessed reunion with Ruth and his Lord Jesus. One of his most memorable quotes in life was, "Someday you will hear that Billy Graham died. Don't you believe a word of it! I shall be more alive then than I am now. I will just have changed my address. I will have gone into the presence of God."[160] The great hope of Christian faith is the promise that there is a new day coming, a new heaven and earth to dawn where there will be no more crying, pain, or death. Those sorrows will forever be gone. I saw Billy for the last time five years ago. As always, he was encouraging and gracious. Even then, however, one could see in his eyes the longing and the hope for life eternal. I'm glad he's gone now to his true and final home.

As I complete this brief story of Billy Graham, I remain full of gratitude for the years of time with him, even though they were minimal compared to those of many others. I am grateful for every brief visit and call and letter. I also think of his evangelistic team, several members of whom are still good friends of mine. Oh, what remarkable people they all are! Christ lives in them, and they exude his character and his love for the world. I quoted this verse early in the book, but it bears repeating. "They are the noble ones in whom is all my delight" (Ps. 16:3).

And before the book ends, in one final chapter, I will appeal to you again to consider the role of Jesus in your life. This is what Billy Graham gave his life to share. I want to tell you about Jesus Christ and give you a final opportunity to commit your life to him. As Billy wrote in his autobiography, "But if through these pages someone learns what it means to follow Christ . . . then the effort has been worth it."[161] That is how I feel too. God bless you richly as you read. I am praying for you as I write these words. I am praying that through these words you will hear the one, holy, loving God of the universe calling you to himself. I pray that you will respond to the call and enter life abundant, now and forever.

TEN

THE MESSAGE OF THE MAN

Come to me, all of you who are weary and carry heavy burdens, and I will give you rest.
—*Matthew 11:28 NLT*

———

My one purpose in life is to help people find a personal relationship with God, which I believe comes from knowing Jesus Christ.

— BILLY GRAHAM[162]

ho is Jesus? Jesus Christ is wonderful. He is beautiful. He is perfect. Let me tell you about him.

First of all, he is God. "The Son is the image of the invisible God, the firstborn over all creation. For in him all things were created: things in heaven and on earth, visible and invisible; . . . all things have been created through him and for him. He is before all things, and in him all things hold together" (Col. 1:15–17). He made you and me and all of creation and declared it good.

Second, Jesus Christ came near and became one of us. "But when the set time had fully come, God sent his son, born of a woman" (Gal. 4:4). We celebrate this fact at Christmas and are drawn to the mystery and wonder of the baby in Bethlehem. But the baby wrapped in swaddling clothes was far more than helpless. As a man, he was majestic. He displayed power over the very forces of nature. Winds and waves obeyed him. He displayed enormous love and concern for all near him. He miraculously fed the hungry. He instantaneously healed diseases. He raised people from death. He powerfully confronted distorted political and religious powers, standing with the oppressed and the abused. Wherever he went he was in charge. For those brief thirty-three years as a man on earth he showed what God's plan was for the world, namely, to make right out of all that is wrong in our world. No evil was in him; no enemies could challenge him. He was God in the flesh, and in command. As those who watched him said, "What kind of man is this? Even the winds and the waves obey him" (Matt. 8:27)!

Finally, Jesus sacrificed enormously to love and rescue all humankind, who can be so twisted, warped, and unlovable. His greatest miracle was to do all that was necessary to rescue us. More on that in a moment.

Who are we?

We are created by God in his image and likeness (Gen. 1:27). That should encourage you! We are therefore full of good longings for purpose, love, contentment, and God himself. And because we are created in his likeness there are times that we are delightful beings. At times, we can be.

But far more often, we are riddled through and through with a lack of goodness and love. We have a spiritual disease that is poisonous and terminal. It is hereditary, according to the Bible. We all have the disease. We were born with it. The best way to describe the signs of the disease is that it causes us to be self-absorbed, selfish to the core, and downright evil toward others in order to get our own way. One moment we can love someone, and the next we can be jealous or slanderous or conniving. We can shock ourselves at times with our thoughts and actions and how they hurt and wound. The word used to describe this condition in the Bible is *sin*.

I remember speaking to a group of middle-school students one time and teaching them about our spiritual disease, but in my teaching, I purposely left out that one word for emphasizing rather our spiritual disease. Then a young girl came to me afterward and said she knew what I meant; I meant "sin." I said to her, "You are right, young lady. The spiritual disease is sin."

She went on, "Mr. Lon, even the spelling of the word 'sin' describes our disease."

I said, "But, how?"

"Well," she said, "because it's got an *I* in the center. Whenever I am the center of life, it's not good. We all have an *I* problem." That's a good way to put it! This was a girl who had learned wisdom in the way the Bible speaks of it in Proverbs 4:

My child, listen carefully
to everything I say.
Don't forget a single word,
but think about it all.
Knowing these teachings
will mean true life
and good health for you. (Prov. 4:20-22 CEV).

The sorrows and the atrocities of human against human throughout history prove this diagnosis. Sin or spiritual disease causes us to hurt others and the world around us. But there is more. The problem is even worse than we think.

God hates sin because sin hurts his creation. He won't stand for sin in his moral universe. He judges it and condemns it. Billy Graham once said, "No sin has escaped the eyes of God." Sin is in us; sin destroys by causing us to pursue selfish ends rather than others' good. Sin is anathema to God. He judges and condemns it.

How can God rescue us? The perfect and holy God who despises and judges sin is the same God who loves us with an extravagant fervor. He is both our judge and lover at the same time. Graham said, "No sin has escaped the eyes of God and no sinner has escaped the love of God." God's love drives him at all costs to rescue us. It was costly beyond all imagination. "But God demonstrates his own love for us in this: While we were still sinners, Christ died for us" (Rom. 5:8). Jesus was born in a cradle. He died on a cross. In that action, he literally took the sin of the whole world upon himself and he died. Why death? Was there no other way? No, there was not. Death is the penalty for sin in a just universe. So, "God made him who had no sin to be sin for us, so that in him we might become the righteousness [right in God's eyes] of God" (2 Cor. 5:21). His sacrifice of death is the means by which you and I can be forgiven of all our sins and made right in his eyes. The enormity of this truth still stuns me. I hope it stuns you too.

There is more. Not only are we forgiven, but if we respond to God's love gift of his life, we can experience his presence in our daily lives. You see, death could not contain him. He rose from death and said to his followers of all ages, "I am with you always, to the end of the age"

(Matt. 28:20). Through his Holy Spirit he now enables us to know him personally. He is with us. Finally, he gives us a promise: He will complete his work of making all things right, and a new heavens and earth will be the final state of his beloved people. We call this heaven, and it gives us one of the all-important human emotion: hope! Forgiveness, relationship, and hope of heaven: gifts from the loving God.

There is only one caveat. This rescue and gift of love is for everyone, but sadly, not everyone receives it. Why? It is only for those who respond to the gift by giving themselves to him in gratitude and humility. Have you ever loved someone but they did not return your love? Probably so. It saddens me to know that many millions of people who hear the love story of Jesus are indifferent or arrogant or self-possessed and say, no thanks. The Bible says, "Everyone who calls on the name of the Lord will be saved" (Rom. 10:9). But you must call on him.

Call on him. I plead with you to call on him. You can do so simply in prayer, by yourself. Prayer is simply talking to God, and he is always listening. Let me suggest a prayer that Billy Graham recommended for decades. It has two dimensions. First, you confess to God that you are a sinner and need his forgiveness. Second, you commit yourself to him and ask him to take charge of your life. If you sense he is calling you to himself, and in your heart you long for him to rescue you and be with you, pray the following prayer:

Dear Lord Jesus,

I know that I am a sinner, and I ask for your forgiveness. I believe you died for my sins and rose from the dead. I turn from my sins and invite you to come into my heart and life. I want to trust and follow You as my Lord [Leader] and Savior [Rescuer]. In Your name, Amen.

Is that all there is? Yes, that's all that is required.** You see, our heart attitude in prayer is more than enough. God looks at the heart. The God who in Christ is calling you is rescuing you as you seek him with all your mind and heart. He promises to never leave or forsake you (see Heb. 13:5). If you have just prayed this prayer for the first time, or you have prayed this prayer in order to recommit your life to God in Christ, I celebrate this moment and this new beginning for you. This is why Billy Graham devoted his life to this message. This is the message of God for all people everywhere for all time.

All my love to you in Christ,

Lon Allison

**P.S. If you just had an encounter with Jesus through prayer please tell someone in the next twenty-four hours. Preferably tell someone who is already a follower of Christ. Ask them to help you understand your spiritual decision and help you start on your forever journey with God.

BIBLIOGRAPHY AND ACKNOWLEDGMENTS

Cornwell, Patricia. *Ruth, A Portrait: The Story of Ruth Bell Graham*. Colorado Springs: Waterbrook, 1998.

Gibbs, Nancy, and Michael Duffy. *The Preacher and the Presidents: Billy Graham in the White House*. New York: Center Street, 2008.

Griffin, William, and Ruth Graham Dinert. *The Faithful Christian: An Anthology of Billy Graham*. New York: McCraken, 1994.

Hanson, Jake. *Igniting the Fire, The Movements and the Mentors Who Shaped Billy Graham*. Uhrichsville, OH: Shiloh Run Press, 2015.

Graham, Billy, Leighton Ford, et al. *Choose Ye this Day: How to Effectively Proclaim the Gospel Message*. Minneapolis: World Wide Publications, 1989.

Graham, Billy. *Just as I Am: The Autobiography of Billy Graham*. New York: HarperCollins, 1997. 2nd ed., 2007.

Graham, Franklin, and Donna Lee Toney, eds. *Billy Graham in Quotes*. Nashville: Thomas Nelson, 2011.

Myra, Harold, and Marshall Shelley. *The Leadership Secrets of Billy Graham*. Grand Rapids, MI: Zondervan, 2008.

Pollock, John. *Billy Graham: The Authorized Biography*. New York: McGraw-Hill, 1966.

Sheets, Dutch. *The Beginner's Guide to Intercessory Prayer*. Grand Rapids, MI: Bethany House, 2008.

Wacker, Grant. *America's Pastor: Billy Graham and the Shaping of a Nation*. Cambridge, MA: Belknap Press of Harvard University Press, 2014.

Whalin, W. Terry. *Billy Graham: A Biography of America's Greatest Evangelist*. New York: Morgan James Faith, 2014.

Special thanks to the Billy Graham Center Archives at Wheaton College, Robert Shuster and Paul Ericksen, scholars, and my colleagues on the journey.
—Lon Allison

NOTES

EPIGRAPHS

1 Billy Graham, preface to *Just as I Am: The Autobiography of Billy Graham* (New York: HarperCollins, 2007), xviii.

2 John Pollock, *Billy Graham: The Authorized Biography* (New York: McGraw-Hill, 1966), 220.

ONE FIRST IMPRESSIONS

3 *Billy Graham, God's Ambassador: A Lifelong Mission of Giving Hope to the World*, compiled by Russ Busby (New York: Time Life Books, 1999), 23.

TWO HOW IT ALL BEGAN

4 Graham, *Just as I Am*, 19.

5 Grant Wacker, *America's Pastor: Billy Graham and the Shaping of a Nation* (Cambridge, MA: Belknap Press of Harvard University Press, 2014), 6.

6 Terry W. Whalin, *Billy Graham: A Biography of America's Greatest Evangelist* (New York: Morgan James Faith, 2014), 11.

7 Graham, *Just as I Am*, 13.

8 Ibid., 16.

THREE THE TIPPING POINT

9 Graham, *Just as I Am*, 29–30.

10 Ibid., 24.

11 Ibid.

12 Whalin, *Billy Graham*, 16.

13 Ibid.

14 Graham, *Just as I Am*, 27.

15 Ibid., 28.

16 Wacker, *America's Pastor*, 6, plus endnote; Graham, *Just as I Am*, 29.

17 See Ed Stetzer, "The State of the American Church," *Evangelical Missions Quarterly*, July 2016, https://emqonline.com/node/3520.

FOUR PREPARING FOR HIS FUTURE

18 *Billy Graham in Quotes*, ed. Franklin Graham and Donna Lee Toney (Nashville: Thomas Nelson, 2011), 115.

19 Ibid., 36.

20 Jake Hanson, *Igniting the Fire: The Movements and Mentors Who Shaped Billy Graham* (Uhrichsville, OH: Shiloh Press, 2015), 35.

21 Graham, *Just as I Am*, 39.

22 Hanson, *Igniting the Fire*, 39.

23 Graham, *Just as I Am*, 41.

24 Ibid., 41.

25 Interview conducted November 14, 2017.

26 Graham, *Just as I Am*, 42.

27 Interview with Jean Ford (Graham), November 14, 2017.

28 Lecture with Lon Allison, North Park Seminary, 1991 or 1992.

29 Whalin, *Billy Graham*, 25.

30 Ibid., 25.

31 Ibid., 27.

32 Hanson, *Igniting the Fire*, 72.

33 Ibid., 73.

34 Ibid.

35 Interview with Jean Ford.

36 Hanson, *Igniting the Fire*, 73.

37 Graham, *Just as I Am*, 6.

38 Hanson, *Igniting the Fire*, 126–27.

39 Discussion with archivist David Malone while I was executive director at the Graham Center at Wheaton.

40 Hanson, *Igniting the Fire*, 151.

41 Whalin, *Billy Graham*, 37.

42 Discussion with David Bruce, Graham's chief of staff.

43 Carl F. George and Warren Bird, *How to Break Church Growth Barriers: Revise Your Role, Release Your People, and Capture Overlooked Opportunities for Your Church* (Grand Rapids, MI: Baker Books, 2017), 21.

44 Interview with missionary scholar Jack Robinson, November 2017.

45 Conversation with Leighton Ford.

46 Hanson, *Igniting the Fire*, 50.

47 Ibid., 72.

48 Ibid., 154.

49 Whalin, *Billy Graham*, 40.

50 Ibid., 43.

51 Leighton Ford tells this story often with mentoring leaders throughout the world.

52 Conversation with Leighton Ford.

FIVE INTIMATE GOD CONNECTION

53 Graham, *Just as I Am*, 155.

54 Interview with Tom Phillips, November 14, 2017.

55 Harold Myra and Marshall Shelley, *The Leadership Secrets of Billy Graham* (Grand Rapids, MI: Zondervan, 2008), 289.

56 Ibid.

57 Letter from David Bruce, December 1, 2017.

58 Interview with Tom Phillips, November 14, 2017.

59 Cliff Barrows related this story to me personally. It has also been recorded on David Edward Pike's blog *Welldigger*, "Billy Graham's Encounter with the Holy Spirit in Wales," March 29, 2012, http://daibach-welldigger .blogspot.com/2012/03/billy-graham-encounters-holy-spirit-in.html.

60 Ibid.

61 Myra and Shelley, *Leadership Secrets*, 23.

62 Graham, *Just as I Am*, 111.

63 Pollock, *Billy Graham*, 79.

64 Ibid., 81.

65 Ibid. Pollock's treatment of this event deserves a full reading by readers who want to know more.

66 Ibid., 91.

67 Ibid., 87.

68 Ibid., 94.

69 Graham, *Just as I Am*, 157–58.

70 Wacker, *America's Pastor*, 13.

71 Ibid., 158.

72 Dutch Sheets, *The Beginner's Guide to Intercessory Prayer* (Grand Rapids, MI: Bethany House, 2008), 24.

73 Pollock, *Billy Graham*, 84.

74 Ibid.

75 Will Graham (Billy's grandson), "Will Graham on Pearl Goode and the Power of Prayer," Billy Graham Evangelistic Association, May 5, 2016, https://billygraham.org/story/will-graham-on-pearl-goode-and-the -power-of-prayer/. See also Cliff Barrows's article, "Passion for Souls, Passion for Prayer," Billy Graham Evangelistic Association, March 29, 2005, https://billygraham.org/decision-magazine/april-2005/passion-for -souls-passion-for-prayer/.

76 Interview with Tom Phillips.

SIX ALL HEAVEN BREAKS LOOSE

77 Graham and Toney, *Billy Graham in Quotes*, 375.

78 Wacker, *America's Pastor*, 21.

79 Graham and Toney, *Billy Graham in Quotes*, back flap.

80 Wacker, *America's Pastor*, 21.

81 Ibid., 255.

82 Ibid., 317.

83 Pollock, *Billy Graham*, 157.

84 Ibid., 167, 178.

85 Ibid., 184.

86 From my own study of response rates of the crusades I attended between 1998 and 2005.

87 Graham, *Just as I Am*, 298.

88 Ibid., 318.

89 Ibid., 321.

90 Ibid., 318.

91 Pollock, *Billy Graham*, 273.

92 Wacker, *America's Pastor*, 21.

93 Ibid., 19.

94 Ibid., 161.

95 Ibid.

96 Pollock, *Billy Graham*, 116.

97 Ibid., 116–18.

98 Wacker, *America's Pastor*, 21.

99 Ibid., 22.

100 Text from David Bruce, December 20, 2017.

101 Graham, *Just As I Am*, 639.

102 Myra and Shelley, *The Leadership Secrets*, 304.

103 Nancy Gibbs and Michael Duffy, *The Preacher and the Presidents: Billy Graham in the White House* (New York: Center Street, 2008), ix.

104 Pollock, *Billy Graham*, 323–24.

105 Myra and Shelley, *Leadership Secrets*, 70–71.

106 Ibid., 210.

107 Graham, *Just as I Am*, 316.

SEVEN RACIAL JUSTICE, PEACE NOT WAR, HUMAN SUFFERING

108 Busby, *Billy Graham, God's Ambassador*, 216.

109 Wacker, *America's Pastor*, 245.

110 Graham, *God's Ambassador*, 212.

111 Discussion with president of Belhaven Roger Parrott, 2007.

112 Graham, *Just as I Am*, 425–26.

113 Ibid., 124.

114 Wacker, *America's Pastor*, 122.

115 Ibid., 426.

116 Ibid., 201.

117 Ibid., 360.

118 Ibid., 696.

119 Pollock, *Billy Graham*, 321.

120 Graham, *Just as I Am*, 430–31.

121 Wacker, *America's Pastor*, 128.

122 Graham, *Just as I Am*, 427.

123 Wacker, *America's Pastor*, 240.

124 Ibid., 239.

125 Ibid., 242.

126 Ibid.

127 Pollock, *Billy Graham*, 117.

128 Ibid., 133.

129 Graham, *Just as I Am*, 438.

130 Ibid., 439.

131 See the Samaritan's Purse website at https://www.samaritanspurse.org/.

EIGHT WEAKNESSES AND REGRETS

132 Graham, *Just as I Am*, 723.

133 Ibid., xxi.

134 Pollock, 75.

135 Ibid., 76.

136 Graham, *Just as I Am*, 723.

137 Ibid., 723–24.

138 Ibid., 724.

139 Ibid.

140 Ibid.

141 Ibid.

142 Ibid., 456.

143 Ibid., 457–58.

144 Wacker, *America's Pastor*, 194–97.

145 Graham, *Just as I Am*, 742.

NINE A SOUL MATE FOR LIFE

146 News release, June 11, 2007, the day before Ruth died.

147 Busby, *Billy Graham*, 231.

148 Ibid., 243.

149 Ruth Bell Graham, *Blessings for a Mother's Day* (Nashville: W Publishing Group, 2001), 120.

150 Patricia Cornwell, *Ruth, A Portrait: The Story of Ruth Bell Graham* (Colorado Springs: Waterbrook, 1998), 181.

151 Whalin, *Billy Graham*, 88.

152 Cornwell, *Ruth*, 186.

153 Ibid., 185, from *Sitting by My Laughing Fire.*

154 Ibid., 184.

155 Ibid., 181.

156 Graham, *God's Ambassador*, 70.

157 Cornwell, *Ruth*, 203.

158 Ibid., 255–57.

159 Ibid., 252–56.

160 Graham, *God's Ambassador*, 274.

161 Graham, *Just as I Am*, xv.

TEN THE MESSAGE OF THE MAN

162 Busby, *Billy Graham*, 1.

ABOUT PARACLETE PRESS

Who We Are

As the publishing arm of the Community of Jesus, Paraclete Press presents a full expression of Christian belief and practice—from Catholic to Evangelical, from Protestant to Orthodox, reflecting the ecumenical charism of the Community and its dedication to sacred music, the fine arts, and the written word. We publish books, recordings, sheet music, and DVDs that nourish the vibrant life of the church and its people.

What We Are Doing

Books

PARACLETE PRESS BOOKS show the richness and depth of what it means to be Christian. While Benedictine spirituality is at the heart of who we are and all that we do, our books reflect the Christian experience across many cultures, time periods, and houses of worship.

We have many series, including *Paraclete Essentials; Paraclete Fiction; Paraclete Giants*; and the new *The Essentials of...*, devoted to Christian classics. Others include *Voices from the Monastery* (men and women monastics writing about living a spiritual life today), *Active Prayer*, the award-winning *Paraclete Poetry*, and new for young readers: *The Pope's Cat*. We also specialize in gift books for children on the occasions of Baptism and First Communion, as well as other important times in a child's life, and books that bring creativity and liveliness to any adult spiritual life.

The MOUNT TABOR BOOKS series focuses on the arts and literature as well as liturgical worship and spirituality; it was created in conjunction with the Mount Tabor Ecumenical Centre for Art and Spirituality in Barga, Italy.

Music

The PARACLETE RECORDINGS label represents the internationally acclaimed choir *Gloriæ Dei Cantores*, the *Gloriæ Dei Cantores Schola*, and the other instrumental artists of the *Arts Empowering Life Foundation*.

Paraclete Press is the exclusive North American distributor for the Gregorian chant recordings from St. Peter's Abbey in Solesmes, France. Paraclete also carries all of the Solesmes chant publications for Mass and the Divine Office, as well as their academic research publications.

In addition, PARACLETE PRESS SHEET MUSIC publishes the work of today's finest composers of sacred choral music, annually reviewing over 1,000 works and releasing between 40 and 60 works for both choir and organ.

Video

Our DVDs offer spiritual help, healing, and biblical guidance for a broad range of life issues including grief and loss, marriage, forgiveness, facing death, understanding suicide, bullying, addictions, Alzheimer's, and Christian formation.

Learn more about us at our website:
www.paracletepress.com
or phone us toll-free at 1.800.451.5006

SCAN
TO
READ
MORE